MAN IN THE MIDDLE

Hall of Famer Ray Lewis' Storied Career with the Ravens

THE BALTIMORE SUN

A tronc Inc. company

Triffon G. Alatzas, Publisher & Editor-in-Chief
Samuel C. Davis, Managing Editor/Audience
Ron Fritz, Senior Editor/Sports
Josh Land, Content Editor/Sports
Andy Knobel, Deputy Sports Editor, Book Editor

Jay Judge, Director of Content/Community News and Market Editor
Leeann Adams, Senior Content Editor/Visuals
Denise Sanders, Photo Technician, Book Photo Editor

Karl Merton Ferron, Cover Photo
Lloyd Fox, Back Cover Photo

Peter J. Clark, Publisher
Molly Voorheis, Managing Editor
Nicky Brillowski, Book and Cover Design
Sam Schmidt, Advertising

ISBN: 978-1-940056-63-0

Printed in the United States of America
KCI Sports Publishing   3340 Whiting Avenue, Suite 5   Stevens Point, WI 54481
Phone: 1-800-697-3756   Fax: 715-344-2668
www.kcisports.com

Legendary Ravens middle linebacker Ray Lewis and daughter Diaymon wave to fans during the Canton Repository Grand Parade of past and 2018 Pro Football Hall of Fame inductees on the Saturday of the annual enshrinement festival in Northeast Ohio. *Lloyd Fox | Baltimore Sun Photo*

CONTENTS

Foreword

BY PETER SCHMUCK · THE BALTIMORE SUN

There is no perfect way to tell The Ray Lewis Story.

Ray certainly isn't perfect and he would be the first to tell you so. He's a dynamic character who is an emotional lightning rod for those who love him and those who don't.

From the depths of his alleged involvement in a double homicide in Atlanta to the heady altitude of his decision to walk off the stage after winning Super Bowl XLVII, his life has been a series of lessons he has applied to himself and attempted to teach others.

Is this a story of redemption?

Of course it is.

Lewis came back from the lowest moment of his life to parlay his football talent into an amazing 17-year career that took him to two Super Bowls, countless individual honors and induction into the Pro Football Hall of Fame in 2018.

Not bad for a guy who was considered an undersized linebacker when he came out of the University of Miami and was the second pick by the Ravens in their very first NFL draft. Lewis and top pick Jonathan Ogden were the defensive and offensive cornerstones of a transplanted franchise that quickly endeared itself to its new fan base.

Is this a story of transformation?

It is clearly so.

Lewis turned his life around after being charged with murder and serving a year's probation for obstruction of justice. He recommitted to his faith and spent countless hours mentoring a generation of young football players to help them avoid the mistakes he made.

On the field, he became a leader well beyond his years and a motivational guru whose pregame speeches turned the Ravens into an adrenaline-fueled machine.

Is this a story of unparalleled excellence?

Who could possibly argue?

The numbers don't lie and neither does his trophy case. Lewis is perhaps the greatest linebacker ever to play the game. He's the only player in NFL history to amass more than 40 sacks and 30 interceptions over the course of his career. He was named NFL Defensive Player of the Year twice and Super Bowl MVP when the Ravens crushed the New York Giants in January 2001.

He went sideline to sideline better than anyone else and recorded so many more combined tackles (1,336) than anyone else in Ravens history that his team record will never be broken ... or even approached.

Is this a story of a personality that bigger than life?

No doubt about it.

His motor never stopped running and neither has his mouth. For better or worse, Lewis continues to inject himself into controversy after controversy, hoping to channel his charisma and street cred into solutions to a number of societal problems.

That has made him a magnet for both criticism and praise, but no one is going to talk Ray Lewis out of being exactly who he is.

Some might say he's full of the spirit. Others might say he's full of himself. No one can say he ever gave less than a full effort to fulfill his destiny and make it into the Hall of Fame.

Perhaps the best way to tell The Ray Lewis Story is to walk beside him throughout his legendary football career with the help of The Baltimore Sun archives. This is his life and career told through the stories, columns and photos of a newspaper staff that has been there for every tackle, every sack and every soliloquy.

This is the story of the greatest Raven of them all. Enjoy. ∎

▸Ray Lewis runs onto the M&T Bank Stadium field before a September 2013 game against the Texans. During a halftime ceremony, he was inducted into the Ring of Honor, which recognizes former players and personnel who made contributions to the Ravens and Colts. *Christopher T. Assaf. | Baltimore Sun Photo*

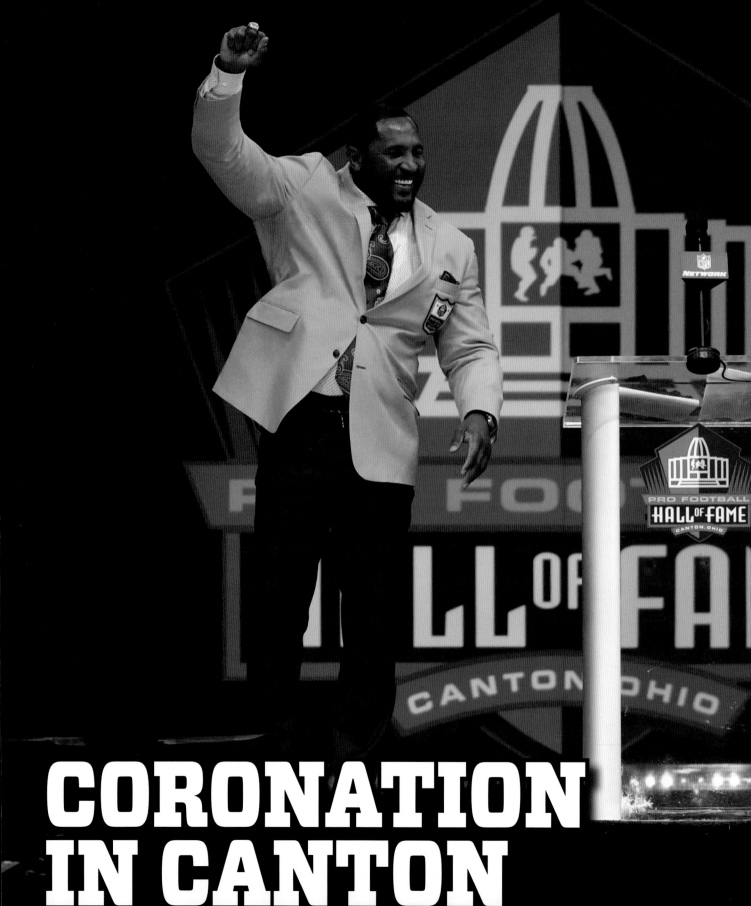

CORONATION IN CANTON

Lewis engages the crowd after unveiling his bust during his 33-minute acceptance speech at Tom Benson Hall of Fame Stadium on the Saturday night of induction weekend. *Lloyd Fox | Baltimore Sun Photo*

Ravens great Ray Lewis is ready for his Hall of Fame close-up

BY CHILDS WALKER · AUGUST 4, 2018 · THE BALTIMORE SUN

When Ray Lewis was a young boy, watching football games with his grandfather on Thanksgiving, he developed an ambition. He wanted to become such a great player that one day, people would talk about him the way his granddad talked about Jim Brown and other legends of the NFL.

On Friday, the day before his enshrinement into the Pro Football Hall of Fame, Lewis got to feel like that little kid again. At a luncheon for the 2018 class and past inductees, the former Ravens great came face to face with Dick Butkus and "Mean" Joe Greene.

Butkus was the great Chicago Bears middle linebacker to whom Lewis was often compared. Greene was the face of the "Steel Curtain" defenses that defined the Pittsburgh Steelers long before they became Lewis' archrivals.

"What I just soaked in for two and a half hours was what I dreamed as a child," Lewis said during a session with reporters after the luncheon. "I have never in my life experienced this level of greatness and this level of respect from people everybody wants to make you compete against. ... But you walk in that room, we're all one."

Later Friday, Lewis would receive the honorary gold jacket given to all Hall of Famers at a ceremonial dinner gathering past inductees.

He'll speak last at the enshrinement ceremony, scheduled to begin at 7 p.m. Saturday night. Fans who didn't make the trip to Canton can watch on ESPN or the NFL Network. Lewis' daughter, Diaymon, will introduce him.

The famously loquacious Lewis said there's "no way" he'll stick to the recommended 15 minutes for his speech. He predicted high emotion over a 22-25-minute talk.

Lewis will anchor a class that includes former Houston Oilers linebacker Robert Brazile, former Washington Redskins executive Bobby Beathard, former Green Bay Packers guard Jerry Kramer, former Chicago Bears linebacker Brian Urlacher, former Philadelphia Eagles safety Brian Dawkins and former Minnesota Vikings wide receiver Randy Moss.

Wide receiver Terrell Owens is also a 2018 inductee, but he chose not to attend the ceremonies this week.

Lewis spoke glowingly of his fellow inductees, from contemporaries such as Urlacher and Dawkins, to old-school linebacker Brazile, whose career he said he recently researched.

"This class, it's a beautiful class from day one," he said. "This is a hard class, a really talented class."

The admiration flowed back toward him.

"I was a fan," Urlacher said of his appreciation for Lewis. "When we played other teams with good players, I was a fan. ... I would stand and watch the other team's defense. I watched Ray."

He joked that when the Bears played the Ravens at Soldier Field in 2005, Lewis blamed him personally for the season-ending injury he suffered in the game, even though they were never on the field at the same time.

"There was a little rivalry there, but I think also mutual respect," Urlacher said.

Brazile said he pulled away from the game for a long time after his career ended.

But he was at his mother's house in Mobile, Ala., one Sunday when she said, "Come here and sit down." On the screen in front of her was a Ravens game.

"See that boy right there, No. 52," she told her son. "He can play."

Brazile took a gander and quickly agreed. "I grew to be a Ray Lewis fan," he said.

Lewis was the second player drafted in Ravens history behind left tackle Jonathan Ogden. Ozzie Newsome selected both in the first round in 1996, the team's initial season in Baltimore.

Ogden went into the Hall of Fame in 2013, a few months after Lewis wrapped up his 17-year career with a victory in Super Bowl XLVII. Now Lewis is

▲From left, safety Brian Dawkins, linebacker Robert Brazile, executive Bobby Beathard, guard Jerry Kramer, wide receiver Randy Moss, Lewis and linebacker Brian Urlacher pose for photos after receiving their gold jackets at the Enshrinees' Gold Jacket Dinner on the Friday night of induction weekend. *Lloyd Fox | Baltimore Sun Photo*

◄Lewis' bust, third from right, is displayed among the others of the 2018 Pro Football Hall of Fame class. *Lloyd Fox | Baltimore Sun Photo*

Lewis soaks in an ovation while taking a lap around the Tom Benson Hall of Fame Stadium field. "I never stopped chasing what being in the Hall of Fame meant," he said. "And now I get it." *Lloyd Fox | Baltimore Sun Photo*

joining him as a first-ballot selection, in Newsome's final season as Ravens general manager no less.

Lewis said he and Ogden smoked cigars together earlier in the week and reminisced about what they accomplished.

"I'm like, 'J.O., we did this,' " he said. "Like, 'Bro, you went in five years ago and now I'm here.' It was a culture that me and him walked in that locker room — and you did not like those locker rooms, trust me — but I tell you what, what we built and what we had, what I have in Baltimore personally, for me to spend my entire 17-year career in Baltimore, that was God's plan."

Other Hall of Famers who played with Lewis on the Ravens include safety Rod Woodson, tight end Shannon Sharpe and cornerback Deion Sanders. Newsome is in the Hall of Fame as a player.

Lewis hopes former Ravens safety Ed Reed will join him in the Hall of Fame next year, Reed's first on the ballot, and that current Ravens linebacker

Terrell Suggs will add to the tally after he retires.

Lewis shared a warm hug with Suggs on the field before Thursday night's Hall of Fame Game between the Ravens and Bears.

"For him to take that leadership, now he's that guy," Lewis said of the player he mentored. "That embrace, it was powerful for me because I watched the youngster that I once raised come up. And now Ed, possibly [going in] next year, it's like me being inducted again."

Lewis said that on the eve of his enshrinement, he felt part of a team that goes beyond the baseline brotherhood between NFL players or former Ravens.

"You can't get cut from this team," he said of the Hall of Fame. "Nobody can move you down from first team to second team. There ain't no, 'I'm better than you, you're better than me.' It does not matter. The only thing that matters is that you're a Hall of Famer." ∎

Lewis does his distinctive dance as he is introduced before the Pro Football Hall of Fame Game between the Ravens and Bears on the Thursday night of induction weekend. The Ravens won the preseason opener, 17-16. *Lloyd Fox | Baltimore Sun Photo*

Ravens fans turn Hall of Fame induction into Baltimore celebration

BY CHILDS WALKER · AUGUST 5, 2018 · THE BALTIMORE SUN

When Ray Lewis arrived in Baltimore 22 years ago, the second-ever draft pick for a franchise with no jersey, no history and no identity, he resolved to build a new football culture in his adopted city.

He succeeded beyond his and his fans' wildest dreams, delivering two Super Bowls, countless fiery stadium entrances and the indelible No. 52 to a town that had felt jilted by the departure of the Colts a dozen years earlier.

So when Lewis arrived in Canton, Ohio, this week to join the hallowed ring of NFL greats in the Pro Football Hall of Fame, he was naturally greeted by many of the Ravens supporters he'd touched. They'd made their way from Maryland in planes, buses and cars, wearing Lewis' colors and his number, hoping to shake his hand and have a cry or a laugh over the times they'd shared.

His induction ceremony Saturday night was a football celebration, but also a Baltimore celebration.

When Lewis stepped out to give the last speech of the night at 9:55 p.m., he began, "Baltimore! Baltimore! We in the building, baby!" The Ravens fans in the announced crowd of 22,205 greeted him with raucous cheers and a rendition of the team's informal theme song, "Seven Nation Army."

Lewis stepped out from behind the lectern and stalked the stage like a preacher, wiping his brow with a black towel. Over the next 33 minutes, he spoke of God, family, team and city.

"I was not the biggest, the strongest, or the fastest," he said as he wrapped up with a broad call for service. "But my goals were clear. My actions were, and still are, in service of those goals. I was a leader on the field then, and I'm a leader in my community now."

Lewis shook his head when the transplanted Cleveland Browns selected him No. 26 overall in the 1996 draft.

"I'm like, 'There is no team in Baltimore,' " he remembered thinking.

But he quickly embraced his role as a chip-on-his-shoulder player for a chip-on-its-shoulder town.

Lewis recalled his outlook.

"I want to show us that we can love each other," he said. "I want to show us that, hey, we may be down and out, but guess what, we will make it out. And that's what those games became, those wars. And that's why I think so many people loved coming to Baltimore games when I was playing. Because whether we won or lost, it did not matter. It was the fight. And that's the way of my city. I love Baltimore as if it's my parents."

These are trying times for the city's sports fans. The Ravens have made the playoffs just once since Lewis retired in 2013, and will begin the 2018 season as an uncertain bet. The Orioles are losing at a near-historic rate, and have shed many of their stars as they attempt to start over.

There's real comfort to be found living in a more glorious past — and no one represents that past more clearly than Lewis, perhaps the greatest middle linebacker in history and the outspoken leader of teams that made the playoffs nine times in his 17 seasons.

"It does bring your mind back toward those times, and it makes you feel good," said 31-year-old Akil Kellar, who traveled to Canton for the induction. "It makes you feel proud to be from Baltimore."

For Kellar, Lewis will always be the man who gave Baltimore football a fresh identity.

►Ravens fans in the announced crowd of 22,205 stand and cheer when Lewis is announced during the Saturday night induction ceremony. He began his speech, "Baltimore! Baltimore! We in the building, baby!" *Lloyd Fox | Baltimore Sun Photo*

"As far as being the face of Baltimore, that's where it started," Kellar said. "For me, Ray Lewis means dedication, hard work and somebody that really gave everything to the game. I felt he's the type of individual who symbolizes the way football is supposed to be played, with toughness and with passion."

"Same thing for me," said 35-year-old Sherree Talley, Kellar's traveling companion. "He's the greatest of all time."

She bumped into Lewis and shook his hand outside the Hall of Fame on Thursday.

"Can't beat that as the highlight of the weekend," she said.

Jeff Ostrow of Baltimore remembered playing pickup basketball with Lewis when he was a newly arrived 21-year-old rookie.

This weekend, Ostrow took his 12-year-old son, Zach, to watch a middle-aged Lewis enter the Hall of Fame.

He marveled at the passage of time.

"Just to see him grow as a player, deal with all his hurdles and then go out winning a Super Bowl, it was awesome," Ostrow said.

Lewis has been a controversial figure for most of his career. He was charged with murder in the deaths of two men outside an Atlanta bar hours after the Super Bowl in 2000. The case against him fell apart and the charges were dropped, but he pleaded guilty to obstruction of justice, a misdemeanor.

Many fans, especially those in other cities, never got past calling him a murderer. More recently, Lewis managed to alienate people on both sides of the NFL's national anthem controversy. He criticized protesting quarterback Colin Kaepernick, and later kneeled with Ravens players as the anthem played before a game in London.

Even this week, social media critics taunted Lewis for grandiose claims he made about reducing crime in Baltimore while he was playing.

But his fans traveled to Canton to celebrate the whole, messy package.

Dave Rather, the owner of Mother's Grille, named a bulldog Fifty-Two in honor of Lewis.

"Back in 2000, we made shirts that said 'Free Ray Lewis,' and I remember we went to a family function, and people were looking at us like, 'How can you support him?' " he said. "A lot of people outside the city just look at him as a murderer and don't want to hear anything else.

"But we in Baltimore know the real story. He paid a pretty big price and since then, he's been a model citizen and helped a lot of people."

Rather drove from Pasadena on Friday with his 12-year-old son, Adam.

Twenty-eight-time Olympic medalist Michael Phelps flew in from Arizona for the ceremony. Phelps was a teenage swimming prodigy living in Rodgers Forge when he befriended Lewis. He'd later lean on the Ravens star for inspiration before Olympic races — and for counsel during difficult times.

"He's a passionate man," Phelps said recently. "He will always be my brother."

On Friday evening, they laughed together at the banquet where an emotional Lewis received the gold jacket he'd wear at his Hall of Fame enshrinement.

Ravens owner Steve Bisciotti chartered a plane so coach John Harbaugh, outside linebacker Terrell Suggs, quarterback Joe Flacco and others from the organization could make it to Canton after practicing in Owings Mills on Saturday morning.

Some fans traveled from more unexpected locales.

Lee Cash of Toronto said he's bled purple, black and gold for 15 years, all because he was drawn to Lewis' rare passion.

"He's just the most incredible specimen I think the NFL has ever had the privilege of having," Cash said. "He's the greatest linebacker, guaranteed. And his persona, his leadership and his faith in God make him a tremendous human being. We love Ray."

Cash's wife surprised him on Valentine's Day with tickets to the Hall of Fame ceremonies, much as she had with playoff tickets during Lewis' last Super Bowl run in 2013.

On Thursday, he got an autograph from Lewis on the back of his No. 52 jersey, and he handed his favorite player a congratulatory box of Montecristo cigars.

Lewis called the turnout for his induction "so overwhelming."

"The buses and you see all of these people coming. ... That's a lifetime with one city," he said. "So it's really overwhelming. But I tell you what, it's so much love, and I give it back in so many ways."

He spoke of sharing a "bigger celebration" with Baltimore when he returns to town after the Hall of Fame enshrinement. He did not offer details.

Lewis made it clear he planned to go past the suggested 10 or 15 minutes for his induction speech Saturday night. He promised to say "thank you" many times over.

Lewis' induction was announced in February. He has spent the time since reflecting on his career.

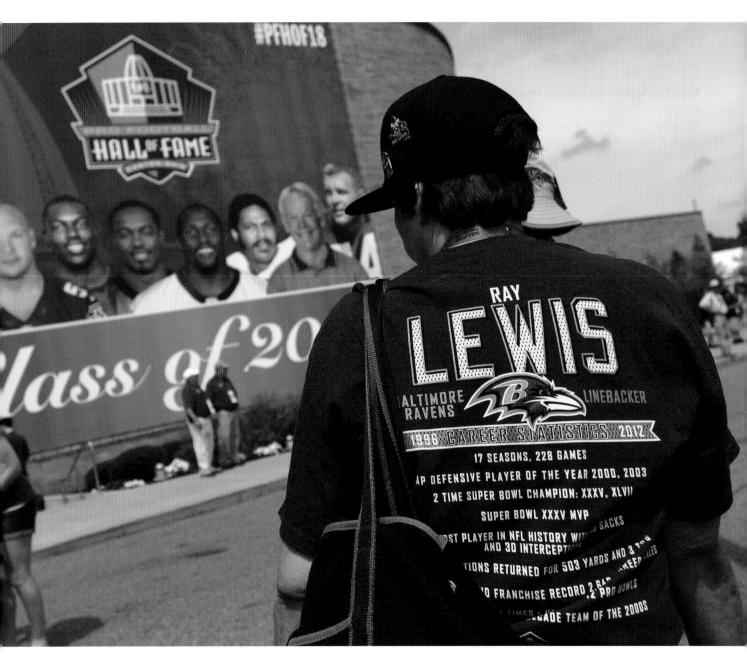

Lewis' achievements are listed on the shirt of an admirer in Canton, Ohio. "You think about the people who helped you through it," he said of overcoming obstacles to reach the Hall of Fame. *Lloyd Fox | Baltimore Sun Photo*

"You really don't think about the good and the bad," he said. "You think about the people who helped you through it."

But he also took his story back to the streets of Lakeland, Fla. As a teenager, he ran mile after mile with Phil Collins singing "In the Air Tonight" on repeat through his headphones.

Lewis described his quest for greatness as a lonely, often selfish, pursuit — but one that ultimately led him to communion with his fans and fellow players.

"I never stopped chasing whatever being in the Hall of Fame meant," he said. "And now I get it." ∎

Newly enshrined Lewis and the Ravens were the 'perfect storm'

BY MIKE PRESTON · AUGUST 5, 2018 · THE BALTIMORE SUN

Ravens middle linebacker Ray Lewis was enshrined among the legends Saturday night, but few of the inductees in the prestigious Pro Football Hall of Fame could match the pageantry or the charisma he displayed throughout his 17-year career.

Lewis socialized and marched among 103 of the Hall of Famers who attended his induction in Canton, Ohio. Now that he has been presented with his gold jacket and had his bust unveiled, he will be remembered forever as one of the best ever to play the game.

But Lewis was more than just a tremendous linebacker. As the consummate professional, he was the total package of an extraordinary player who showed great leadership. His strong work ethic was a result of his overwhelming fear of failure.

He was the master entertainer who never met a camera he didn't like.

"We have tissues in the bag for this," said Roberta Donahue, 57, who drove from Eldersburg with her husband, Jeff, to watch the induction. "He's the greatest football player and we've watched all his games. He has always been an entertainer with playmaking abilities. The leadership showed throughout his entire career."

Every player in Canton has been recognized for his play, but some took the game to another level. Quarterback Johnny Unitas and the Baltimore Colts brought the NFL into TV households when they beat the New York Giants in the 1958 title game, dubbed "The Greatest Game Ever Played."

Quarterback Joe Namath gave the American Football League instant credibility when his New York Jets upset the Colts in Super Bowl III in January 1969.

And now Baltimore is back in Canton again with Lewis.

"It was the perfect storm," said Matt Shannon, 40, a Ravens fan who lives in Columbus, Ohio.

Lewis didn't have the impact of a Unitas or Namath, but he gave the Ravens instant credibility. Former Ravens offensive tackle Jonathan Ogden, inducted into the Hall of Fame in 2013, is the greatest player in team history, but Lewis became the face of an organization that has become one of the league's best.

That wasn't the case in 1995. The move from Cleveland to Baltimore made the Ravens the most hated team in the NFL. They had no logo, no team colors and no tradition. Worse yet, they had almost no money.

But Lewis gave the franchise energy because of his magnetic and colorful personality. He gave the Ravens swagger and eventually two Super Bowl titles — after the 2000 and 2012 seasons.

"People knew the Ravens because of my dad," said his daughter, Diaymon, who introduced Lewis at the Hall of Fame ceremony.

▸Lewis, with daughter Diaymon, acknowledges fans during the Canton Repository Grand Parade. "People knew the Ravens because of my dad," said Diaymon, who introduced her father during the induction ceremony the next night. *Lloyd Fox | Baltimore Sun Photo*

And then there was the "Squirrel" dance, possibly the greatest player introductory dance in pro sports.

"The dance was cool, awesome," Donahue said. "That dance got everyone going and it was perfect for the start of every home game."

"People would like to see Sugar hit that thang," said Lewis of his dance Saturday night.

Those are the things that transcended Lewis' play on the field. He had that charisma, the showmanship and the wardrobe that put him in line with other Hall of Famers such as Deion Sanders, Deacon Jones and Namath.

Lewis was Showtime. He brought that endless amount of energy Saturday night, moving and jumping on stage. Lewis was the only inductee who wore a wireless microphone as he gave thanks to his teammates, former coaches and family members.

"Few players can bridge that gap from athlete to entertainer," Shannon said. "I grew up a Browns fan, but I followed the team when they moved to Baltimore. I have stuff chucked at me, peanuts thrown at me when I go back [to Cleveland] for a game. Browns fans are terrible. Ray became the face of the team and has started since day one, he and J.O. It was a new team, new defensive mindset and it was all great."

The rest of the nation has had a chance to get more of a firsthand look at Lewis this week. He has been humble at times but also arrogant. He has preached, and yet gone on some of his silly rants that make no sense.

That's vintage Ray Lewis.

Regardless, his teammates have always admired and respected him. With Lewis, he could talk the talk and then back it up. And then he would get his teammates to believe they could pull off similar miracles. He would "lay hands" on Jacoby Jones and make him believe he could return a kickoff for a touchdown. He did. Twice in 2012.

He could sit next to running back Jamal Lewis on the bench and tell him that "this game belonged to the Lewis boys" and Jamal Lewis would break off a 60-yard rush. Those moments aren't just fantasy but documented.

Besides the two Super Bowl titles, Ray Lewis was selected to the Pro Bowl 13 times and was the league's Defensive Player of the Year twice. Eight times he finished a season with more than 100 tackles.

During Lewis' time in Baltimore, four of the Ravens defensive coordinators became head coaches. Since he retired after the 2012 season, the Ravens have been to the playoffs only once.

Best hits?

There are too many to rate.

Best moments?

"He was just exceptional on the field," said Dave Adams, 46, of Hanover, Pa. "There were many hits, the two Super Bowls, the final ride — all were special. We came here five years ago for J.O. and we decided then that we were going to come back when Ray got in. He had outstanding leadership, and he made everybody better."

Lewis' home was often the meeting place for other players to study film during the middle of the week. He practiced like he played and his offseason workouts at Oregon Ridge were legendary.

Near the end of Lewis' career, Ravens coach John Harbaugh had to speak to him about slowing down in practice and saving himself for the games on Sundays.

He was a totally committed player.

Earlier this week at a breakfast with former Colts running back Lenny Moore, Lewis thanked him and others such as Jim Brown for paving the way for African-American players.

He has complimented and been compared to Chicago Bears legendary middle linebacker Dick Butkus and admired the leadership of Pittsburgh Steelers defensive tackle "Mean" Joe Greene.

But Saturday night was Lewis' moment. Those Ravens fans in attendance had forgotten anything Lewis might have said or done in the past.

"Ray is Ray," Shannon said laughing. "I think it was Joe Flacco who said he listens to Ray speak and never understands what he is saying. I agree. He says some crazy stuff sometimes. But I would run through a wall every time I'd hear him say something. He is a great motivator and was great for the game, as well as the Ravens."

And that's why he was paid the ultimate tribute Saturday. ∎

▶ Lewis can't hold back tears after he is given his gold jacket at the Enshrinees' Gold Jacket Dinner at the Memorial Civic Center and Cultural Center. "We have tissues in the bag for this," fan Roberta Donahue of Eldersburg said of preparing for the weekend. *Lloyd Fox | Baltimore Sun Photo*

Prowling and howling through a 33-minute thank-you speech

BY CHILDS WALKER · AUGUST 5, 2018 · THE BALTIMORE SUN

Ray Lewis prowled the stage for all 33 minutes of a sprawling Hall of Fame induction speech Saturday night, taking listeners on a tour of his childhood and playing career before concluding with a call for community service.

The Ravens great pointed out dozens of family members, friends, coaches and former teammates in the announced crowd of 22,205, thanking them for helping him fulfill an unlikely destiny as one of the finest defenders in NFL history.

Lewis, clad in purple pants and a matching purple and gold tie, received a raucous ovation from Baltimore fans as he took the stage at Tom Benson Hall of Fame Stadium in Canton, Ohio. He began his speech, the last of the night, almost three hours later, at 9:55 p.m.

His daughter, Diaymon, introduced him, saying: "People knew the Ravens because of my dad. ... Everything he knew, everything he lived for was through the Ravens."

Lewis began by talking about the hard times and hopes he shared with his mother, Sunseria Smith, who gave birth to him at age 15.

"Remember what they told me when we were little?" he said, addressing Smith in the crowd. "That we weren't gonna make it. Well guess what, Mama? We made it."

He remembered how Smith tried to move the family to Tennessee when he was in 11th grade. But he believed his destiny lay in Florida. His mother sent him back with $39 and $20 in food stamps.

"I'll make it," he recalled telling her.

He said the University of Miami gave him its last scholarship, an opportunity no other big-time program offered.

When the narrative reached his NFL home, he asked his fellow 1996 Ravens first-round draft pick, Jonathan Ogden, to stand, and he incited the crowd with a long chant of "Baltimore! Baltimore! Baltimore!"

He praised the team's original owner, the late Art Modell, as a "visionary" and one of the many father figures in his life.

Current Ravens owner Steve Bisciotti chartered a plane to fly coach John Harbaugh and seven players — linebackers Terrell Suggs and C.J. Mosley, quarterback Joe Flacco, guard Marshal Yanda, punter Sam Koch, long snapper Morgan Cox and kicker Justin Tucker — to Canton after they practiced in Owings Mills on Saturday morning.

General manager Ozzie Newsome, who drafted Lewis No. 26 overall in 1996, sat on stage in his gold jacket with the rest of the 140 Hall of Fame members who greeted their seven new fellows (wide receiver Terrell Owens opted not to attend and held his own ceremony in Chattanooga, Tenn., on Saturday afternoon).

A cross-section of Lewis' former teammates, from possible 2019 Hall of Fame selection Ed Reed to previous inductees Shannon Sharpe, Rod Woodson and Ogden, also attended.

Lewis' friend, 28-time Olympic

Lewis is called to the stage during the induction ceremony Saturday night. Lewis, wearing purple pants and a purple and gold tie, delivered a rollicking, emotional account of his personal life and professional career.
Lloyd Fox | Baltimore Sun Photo

swimming medalist Michael Phelps, sat near the front of the crowd with his wife, Nicole.

"How many times have we sat in a room together?" he said, addressing a tearful Phelps directly. "What did we say? 'We'll do anything for Baltimore!' A lot of people call you the greatest Olympian, but I call you one of my greatest friends, brother."

Former Pittsburgh Steelers running back Jerome Bettis offered a tribute to his former rival: "Ray was a great athlete. He was fast, all that. But what was really great about Ray is that he was able to get his entire team to play with the energy and passion he played with."

Before Lewis spoke, 82-year-old Jerry Kramer drew laughs from the Baltimore fans when he recalled an early 56-0 whipping his Green Bay Packers took from the Colts, who released a white horse to gallop every time they scored.

"We damn near killed him," quipped Kramer, the oldest member of the 2018 class.

In narrating his career, Lewis harped on his final season, when his triceps "popped off the bone" in the sixth game of the regular season. He said a team physician told him no one had ever come back from such an injury in the course of one season.

"That was like pouring lighter fluid on an open flame," he said.

Lewis had already privately decided the season would be his last, and he had no intention of finishing it on injured reserve. He said he called Newsome to tell him as much the next day.

He returned for the playoffs and concluded his career with a goal-line stand to clinch his second Super Bowl victory.

Lewis also obliquely addressed the runup to the 2000 season, when he was charged with murder in connection with the deaths of two men outside a Super Bowl party he attended in Atlanta.

Though the charges were ultimately dropped, he called those "some of the darkest moments of my life." But he used the reference as another opportunity to thank the people who stuck by him.

"I tell you something," he said. "God sends you a family that makes sure you're OK when you're going through what you're going through." ■

►Legendary Ravens left tackle Jonathan Ogden (left), who was inducted into the Hall of Fame in 2013, joins Lewis onstage for a rendition of the latter's famed "Squirrel" dance. The Ravens selected both players in the first round of the NFL draft in 1996. *Lloyd Fox | Baltimore Sun Photo*

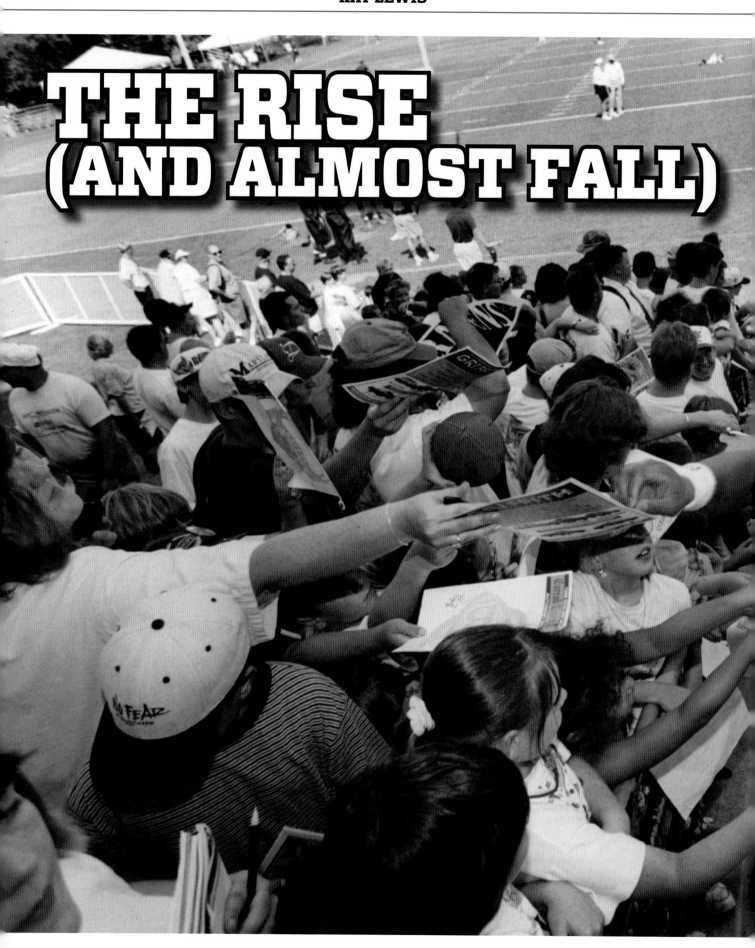

THE RISE
(AND ALMOST FALL)

Ray Lewis signs autographs on the first day of training camp in July 1996 in Westminster. *John Makely | Baltimore Sun Photo*

Ravens thankful Miami linebacker Lewis falls to them in draft at pick No. 26

BY GARY LAMBRECHT · APRIL 21, 1996 · THE BALTIMORE SUN

The Ravens were determined to come away from the first round of the NFL draft with a linebacker, and they were pleasantly surprised that former Miami star Ray Lewis was available when it was their turn to take the 26th pick.

Baltimore, which lost a chance to get Kevin Hardy when Jacksonville landed him as the overall second pick, didn't let Lewis get away. The Ravens only hope Lewis develops with them as quickly as he did at Miami, where he established himself as a freshman middle linebacker in 1993, and went on to have three solid seasons.

Lewis, 6 feet, 235 pounds, isn't especially big for his position. But in coach Ted Marchibroda's mind, the proof is on the film. There, Marchibroda saw a guy who relentlessly fought through blocks and pursued ball carriers and had the kind of speed to run them down from all angles. Then, there is Lewis' demonstrative demeanor.

"He has the football temperament that we were looking for. When you watch him on film, he catches your eye, and you love to watch him play," Marchibroda said. "He was a guy we didn't think would fall this far, but we're thankful that he did. He's going to be a big help in an area where we had to have it."

The Ravens, who considered taking running back Leeland McElroy or tight end Jason Dunn before choosing Lewis, see him as a versatile type who can play outside in their base 4-3 alignment or move inside in the 3-4 set.

"He commands respect when he steps into the huddle. He's all business. He knows what his profession is, and he's going to attack it. He's very much like Greg Lloyd," said Ravens defensive coordinator Marvin Lewis, who coached linebackers for the Pittsburgh Steelers before coming to Baltimore. "As a young player, he was a great player at Miami. He wasn't intimidated. He intimidated people with his attitude and persona."

In three seasons with the Hurricanes, Lewis made 388 tackles, fifth on the school's career list. In 1993, he became the first freshman to start for Miami in five years, and had 76 tackles. As a junior last year, he was a consensus first-team All-America choice after making 160 tackles (95 solo).

"The way I play the game is like a dog," Lewis said. "You take food away from a dog and run from him, he's going to come and get you. That's the way I play when a man has the ball in his hands.

"I just love to play the game. I love the competition, just being out there sweating, trying to beat the next man in front of you."

It was a day of mixed emotions for Lewis. Hours before being drafted, he attended the funeral of former Hurricanes teammate and roommate Marlin Barnes, who was slain last week.

"Right now, all I can do is be happy," Lewis said. "I know he is looking down on me, smiling right now." ∎

▶The Ravens introduce Lewis (foreground), one of their first-round draft picks, to the media in 1996. Defensive coordinator Marvin Lewis (middle) and Lewis' agent, Drew Rosenhaus (most distant), attend the news conference. *Gene Sweeney Jr. | Baltimore Sun Photo*

Lewis gets his first NFL sack as he takes down future teammate Jim Harbaugh in a 26-21 road loss to the Colts in October 1996. Harbaugh's brother, John, later coached the Ravens. *Gene Sweeney Jr. | Baltimore Sun Photo*

DRAFT
Analysis

BY MIKE PRESTON · APRIL 22, 1996 · THE BALTIMORE SUN

[Director of football operations Ozzie] Newsome will be second-guessed for taking Miami linebacker Ray Lewis over Texas A&M running back Leeland McElroy with the team's second choice in the first round, No. 26 overall.

But the decision was logical.

The Ravens entered the draft with only one proven linebacker in Pepper Johnson. Linebacker Craig Powell was the team's No. 1 pick a year ago, but he's coming off a knee injury.

In Lewis, the Ravens get a speedy and physical inside linebacker who was generally rated No. 1 in the draft. Johnson, Powell, and Lewis could be a solid trio. ∎

▶Lewis encourages the crowd to cheer after the Ravens stop the Eagles on fourth-and-1 in an August 1996 preseason victory. *John Makely | Baltimore Sun Photo*

Top picks Ogden, Lewis instantly invaluable as rookies

BY GARY LAMBRECHT · NOVEMBER 8, 1996 · THE BALTIMORE SUN

They did not perform like typical freshmen as college players, and as first-year players in the NFL, left guard Jonathan Ogden and inside linebacker Ray Lewis do not seem like rookies anymore.

Then again, the consensus in the Ravens' locker room is that Ogden and Lewis never were looked upon as rookies in the first place. Judging by the responsibilities they have handled as the top two picks in the Ravens' inaugural draft, Ogden and Lewis are growing up fast, indeed.

Consider that a little more than halfway through their rookie seasons, they already are fixtures on offense and defense, having started every game. One probably has to go back to the organization's 1978 draft, when the Cleveland Browns selected linebacker Clay Matthews and a tight end named Ozzie Newsome in the first round, to find a pair of players who have had such an immediate impact.

Take Ogden. As the fourth player chosen, out of UCLA, he was far and away the best offensive lineman available in the draft – not to mention the most imposing at 6 feet 8, 320 pounds.

"He's one of those guys who has the ability and intelligence to play any position on the line we asked him to play," coach Ted Marchibroda said. "He's done the job all year."

The transition for Lewis has not been quite as smooth, for several reasons.

Before training camp, the Ravens released 10-year veteran middle linebacker Pepper Johnson and handed the keys to the 4-3 defense over to Lewis, the 26th overall pick in the draft.

That's a lot to ask of any rookie, even a guy who was among the nation's top linebackers for three stellar seasons at Miami, where Lewis recorded 17 tackles in his first game as a true freshman and never looked back during an All-America career.

Then there is Lewis' size. At 6-1, 235, he has run into his share of problems taking on linemen and blocking backs who bring more beef to the battle than Lewis provides. And it hasn't helped that the defensive line – which should keep blockers off Lewis – has been ravaged by injuries.

"Nobody walks into this league and becomes an All-Pro in one minute, and Ray understands that he's going through growing pains," said linebackers coach Maxie Baughan. "We put a lot of faith in Ray to start with. He's responded by giving us everything we've wanted from him. He's played as well and as hard as he can play."

Lewis' instincts and quickness to the ball, particularly in lateral pursuit, have been impressive since the season opener, when he earned Defensive Player of the Week honors in a 19-14 victory over the Oakland Raiders. He leads the Ravens with 92 tackles, 67 solo, and he has added four pass deflections and an interception.

He has tailed off a bit in recent weeks, although Lewis, who has never stopped hustling, dismissed fatigue as a factor in his rookie year.

"Everybody keeps talking about hitting the wall, but I don't believe in that," Lewis said. "You set your mind for whatever your job requires. I've set my mind for a 16-game season. I knew I was one of the top draft picks, so I had to set my mind to

Lewis (left) celebrates with safety Stevon Moore after intercepting a pass in the end zone in the Ravens' first game, a 19-14 home win against the Raiders in September 1996. *Kenneth K. Lam | Baltimore Sun Photo*

knowing I was going to play more. I've got my nicks and bruises. Other than that, I'm all right." Marchibroda said the same thing about Ogden and Lewis.

"We probably placed too much of a burden on Ray as the signal caller, and he's had more of a learning process to go through," Marchibroda said. "They are both exactly what we thought they would be. They both enjoy the game, they both enjoy practice, and they're both talented athletes. They're special people." ∎

Lewis a rock for a team on shaky ground

BY JOHN EISENBERG · NOVEMBER 16, 1997 · THE BALTIMORE SUN

Ray Lewis and Jerome Bettis ran into each other socially last weekend in Pittsburgh before the Ravens played the Steelers.

"You know I'm gonna be coming," said Bettis, the Steelers' powerful running back.

"And you know I'm going to be waiting," responded Lewis, the Ravens' middle linebacker.

The Steelers mauled the Ravens the next night, but Lewis made good on his promise. He was waiting for Bettis – and for any other Steeler who wandered into his jurisdiction.

Finishing with 14 unassisted tackles and three assists, including a memorable slam-dunk of the 245-pound Bettis on a run up the middle, Lewis was the sole bright light for the Ravens on a dark night.

It was a signature performance by a young player emerging as a force, a playmaker, a leader – everything the Ravens, or any team, could want from a middle linebacker.

Lewis (left) and fellow linebackers Mike Caldwell (56) and Keith Goganious attempt to tackle Steelers running back Jerome Bettis (36) in a 31-17 home win in December 1996. *Jeffrey F. Bill | Baltimore Sun Photo*

"He reminds me of Greg Lloyd," said Ravens defensive coordinator Marvin Lewis, invoking the name of the Steelers' All-Pro linebacker. "Greg asks me about Ray every time we play, which is quite a compliment. I think Greg sees himself in Ray, too."

A 1996 first-round draft pick from the University of Miami, Lewis, 22, is already on the short list of the NFL's best young defenders.

What tackle Jonathan Ogden is on offense for the Ravens – the franchise – Lewis is becoming on defense.

"You have a choice – either you're going to be an average player in the NFL or one of the great ones," Lewis said. "Either you just play and pick up your paycheck every Monday, or you become known as a great football player. I want that."

His numbers suggest he is delivering "that" and more this season. He has made 108 unassisted tackles and assisted on 32 others in 10 games, for an astounding average of 14 tackles a game.

His totals are higher than the combined totals of the Ravens' second- and third-best tacklers, Stevon Moore and Michael McCrary.

Ravens coach Ted Marchibroda (white shirt) and Lewis (do-rag) address the team after practice in August 1997.
John Makely | Baltimore Sun Photo

With three tackles in today's game against the Philadelphia Eagles at Memorial Stadium, Lewis would surpass his total for last season, when he led the Ravens in tackling as that rarest of football creatures, a starting rookie middle linebacker.

It's simply a fact that Lewis is making more and more plays, and missing fewer and fewer.

"Ray did a good job last year," Marvin Lewis said, "but this year he has a much better understanding of the different offenses he is facing every week, and what his role is in stopping them."

The player agrees wholeheartedly with his coach.

"The big change for me [from 1996] is studying and focusing," Ray Lewis said. "I like to go home, sit downstairs by myself and just study film alone.

"You can read things when you're alone. You can just focus on the field and learn the formations. And then I see the formations on Sunday and I know what's coming. It's easy."

That's experience?

"And maturity," Marvin Lewis said. "Ray also is more prepared physically. A lot of first-year players need that first offseason to develop after they get here [to the NFL] and realize how tough and physical it is. Ray was one of the guys who was here early every morning and every day during the offseason."

But the cold calculation of big statistics, weight work and study habits still doesn't illustrate Lewis' energetic playing style. He is a shouter, a fist thrower, a trash talker; the Raven most likely to bounce off a teammate and give an animal yell after a big hit. You can sense his intensity from the worst seats in the house.

"I'm having fun," Lewis said. "It's like when you're a kid out playing in the yard and you're just wanting to make all the plays and have fun. That's what I'm doing." ∎

Lewis becomes highest-paid middle linebacker at $26 million

BY MIKE PRESTON · NOVEMBER 20, 1998 · THE BALTIMORE SUN

Nearly two weeks ago in practice at the Ravens' training complex in Owings Mills, team owner Art Modell pulled middle linebacker Ray Lewis aside and chatted with him on a golf cart.

Modell asked Lewis to name the top five linebackers in the NFL, and as Lewis finished his list, Modell promised him that he would become the highest paid of the group.

Last night, Modell delivered, as Lewis signed a four-year contract extension worth $26 million, which included a $7 million signing bonus, making him the NFL's highest-paid middle linebacker, as well as one of the top five defensive players in the league in salary.

According to Lewis, the team's leading tackler the past three years, the language of the contract was finalized yesterday morning. He signed shortly after meeting with Modell following practice and a team meeting.

"He said he was definitely going to take care of me, and as far as I'm concerned, he's a man of his word," Lewis said of Modell. "I don't know what he's told anyone else, but I know what he told Ray Lewis and he came through.

There will be no more, 'He's this, he's that, he's underpaid.' There will be no more of that. I wanted to stay here because I love this team, the players and this city."

Modell said he had no problems paying Lewis

Lewis sits with his mother, Sunseria Keith in Lewis' Reisterstown home in June 1998.
Lloyd Fox | Baltimore Sun Photo

an average of $6.5 million per season because he rated Lewis the best in the game, and better than any other linebacker who has played for his franchise in Cleveland or Baltimore.

Modell said his passion for the game sets Lewis apart from other players.

"This organization has rewarded Ray Lewis for a job well done and the job to be done for many, many years to come," Modell said. "This is a reflection of the Modell family and the organization because we want to protect the hard-core players on our team, the producers on our team, people that excel at what they do.

"This season has been tough and it's unlike

something we have experienced often in this organization. Ray Lewis loves to hit. He has speed and a passion for the game which separates the men from the boys. He's been loyal to this organization. This is a commitment to our future."

Lewis is the team's leading tackler for the third straight season with 79. He had 142 tackles in 1996 and led the league with 210 last year when he was named to the AFC's Pro Bowl squad.

Asked if he was going home to celebrate, Lewis said yes, and he intended to party with his mother.

"She has been on her knees praying for me a long time," he said. ∎

Lewis displays in June 1998 the Mackey Award he received from the NFLPA as Linebacker of the Year. *Lloyd Fox | Baltimore Sun Photo*

On top in the middle: Lewis considered NFL's best middle linebacker

BY MIKE PRESTON · DECEMBER 12, 1999 · THE BALTIMORE SUN

Ask Ravens middle linebacker Ray Lewis about his favorite hit, and his eyes light up and he flashes a grin.

"The best hits always come under fire and nobody sees them, like when you hit a running back so hard his eyes roll back in his head. I've had a couple of those," Lewis said. "Eddie George [Tennessee Titans running back] and I are very good friends off the field. A couple of weeks ago, I came off a block and hit Eddie as he came through the hole.

"His eyes kind of rolled back, and he just sat there on the field. The only thing I said to him was, `Hey, Eddie, it's just me, Ray.' "

Two years ago, players in the league took notice of Lewis when he was named to the AFC Pro Bowl squad as one of the conference's best middle linebackers.

Now, there are coaches as well as peers who believe he is the best in the NFL.

"People talk about him running side to side, making tackles, knocking balls down, picking them off," Tennessee coach Jeff Fisher said of Lewis, 24. "But he is a smart player. I think he is one of the smartest right now playing the position, recognizing formations and keys. I think he is playing as good as anyone in the league right now."

Arguments could be made for several others as the best, including the Tampa Bay Buccaneers' Hardy Nickerson and Atlanta Falcons' Jessie Tuggle, but both are 34 and on the downside of their careers.

The Miami Dolphins have Zach Thomas and the Pittsburgh Steelers offer 270-pound Levon Kirkland.

Tenth-year player Junior Seau of the San Diego Chargers is often mistaken for a middle linebacker, but he really plays weak side.

Even including Seau, none of those players has had more tackles or is required to do more in their overall schemes than Lewis. From 1996 to 1998, Thomas had 362 solo tackles, Kirkland 264 and Seau 286. Lewis had 386. This year, he has 107 solo tackles. Add his 50 assists, and he has a league-leading 157 total tackles.

"Ray can make tackles from sideline to sideline," said Jacksonville Jaguars right guard Zach Wiegert. "He can rush the passer. He can cover people. He's just an all-around player. He's the best linebacker I've played against."

'He covers a lot of room'

"His biggest asset is speed," said Buffalo Bills quarterback Doug Flutie, possibly the game's most elusive quarterback. "That's what I saw and I don't have to get up in his face and block him. He is at the middle linebacker position, but has the agility of a defensive back."

Lewis can't remember his time in the 40-yard dash, but it was 4.5 seconds coming out of college. He doesn't take his speed for granted, either. Lewis hired a personal trainer two years ago, and works out at a stadium in Orlando, Fla., in the offseason.

A typical routine consists of running the entire stadium steps with a 50-pound body suit. He then runs 15 to 20 100-yard sprints before taking off the added weight and going through his usual pass drops and other drills.

"By that time, I can fly," said Lewis, who tells

▶Lewis leaves the field at Memorial Stadium after a 42-34 loss to the Steelers in October 1997.
John Makely. | Baltimore Sun Photo

quarterbacks, "I'll be back," after each sack. "I've always been the one to live off speed. In the offseason, I build power and work hard to maintain speed. That's something I don't want to lose. As long as the Lord continues to bless me with speed, I can play this game."

Room to improve

Ask Lewis who the best middle linebacker in the NFL is, and without hesitation, he says, "Me."

Lewis wants to make every tackle, which is a strength as well as a weakness. He has made major improvement in his pass coverage in the past three years, but still needs more work in that area.

Ravens defensive coordinator Marvin Lewis says that will come with practice, age and repetition. Ray Lewis isn't afraid of work. He is as relentless in practice as he is on game day. Ravens coach Brian Billick had to tone him down in training camp.

"He is a great practice player," said defensive coordinator Marvin Lewis, who has coached Lewis since his rookie season. "Ray is a leader. People attract to him. They did at the University of Miami, they did from day one here, even with veteran players. Some players don't want that responsibility; Ray does.

"Ray has the desire to make every single tackle on the field. Sometimes that gets him in trouble because he tries to cover for other people, tries to do too much. When he matures more and realizes that he can't make every play, he'll end up making just about all of them."

Ray Lewis likes to be challenged. If he doesn't make at least 10 tackles a game, it irritates him.

"People around me know that I come to play on Sundays," he said. "But I also realize that I'm just getting started. The day you say you're at your peak, then you're saying you're satisfied. I've got a lot more to do."

That means the best is going to get better. ■

▶Lewis (52) and free safety Rod Woodson tackle wide receiver Courtney Hawkins during a 23-20 home loss to the Steelers in 1999. *Lloyd Fox | Baltimore Sun Photo*

Lewis charged with murdering two men near Atlanta bar after night of Super Bowl parties

BY MIKE PRESTON · FEBRUARY 1, 2000 · THE BALTIMORE SUN

Ravens linebacker Ray Lewis was charged with first-degree murder last night in the stabbing deaths of two men outside an Atlanta nightclub in the early morning after a night of Super Bowl parties.

In arresting Lewis, Atlanta police said he was suspected of being one of several men who fled the scene of the killings in a limousine.

Earlier yesterday, Lewis told The Sun that he had been cleared by Atlanta police to leave the city, and he had been expected to fly to Hawaii this morning for the Pro Bowl game Sunday.

Ravens coach Brian Billick said the team would issue no statement until after Lewis, 24, appears in Atlanta Municipal Court, which he was expected to do at 8 a.m. today.

Lewis' attorney, Carey Deeley, declined to comment last night.

"He is in our custody," said Atlanta police spokesman John Quigley.

The two men were stabbed to death in Atlanta's Buckhead entertainment district. Witnesses said six men who had fought with them left the scene in a black Lincoln Navigator limousine leased by Lewis and that several shots were fired from inside the vehicle.

The Atlanta Journal-Constitution reported that several detectives and policemen had placed Lewis inside the vehicle as it sped away from the crime scene. Atlanta police said the limousine had Maryland license plates and was leased from All-Stretched Out Limousine Service, a Baltimore company. The owner of the company was unavailable for comment last night.

Lewis was the only person who had been charged in the slayings by late last night, police said.

The victims were identified by the Atlanta medical examiner's office as Richard Lollar, 24, and Jacinta Baker, 21, both of Decatur, Ga. Both were believed to have been partying in the area. Baker was pronounced dead at the scene shortly after the 4 a.m. fight, and Lollar died later at Grady Memorial Hospital.

According to a published report, detectives found the stretch limousine behind a Holiday Inn on Peachtree Road near Lenox Mall. Homicide detectives spent most of the day talking to the driver but would not provide details.

Police were called to the hotel after someone told them that a man with bloodstains on his clothing had gotten out of the limousine and entered a bathroom in the hotel lobby to wash, officers said.

Earlier in the day, Lewis had little to say about the incident.

"I cooperated fully," Lewis told The Sun. "As for the situation, I have no comment."

Lewis and his agent, Roosevelt Barnes, had said that the former University of Miami standout was not a suspect. "He is not involved in any aspect of this investigation as far as I know," Barnes told the Atlanta Journal-Constitution.

Ravens owner Art Modell had said earlier in the day, "I don't believe he had anything to do with it. I'm going to give Ray the benefit of the doubt and defend him until something is proven otherwise."

Police believe the argument began at the Cobalt Lounge, the scene of a fatal shooting two weeks ago that left a Marietta, Ga., man dead.

Lewis had become the team's most popular player on and off the field. But privately, team officials and teammates had become concerned about new friends he had made.

Defense attorneys Ed Garland (left) and Don Samuel flank Lewis as he pleads guilty to the charge of misdemeanor obstruction of justice in June 2000 in Fulton County (Ga.) Superior Court. *AP Photo*

On Dec. 6, assault charges were filed against Lewis stemming from an incident in a Baltimore County bar.

According to a police report, Catrice Parker, 24, of Baltimore claimed Lewis struck her on the left side of her face and she fell into the bar at the Windsor Mill Inn in the 7200 block of Windsor Mill Road. Lewis was expected to stand trial Feb. 9 in Catonsville.

Ravens officials had been expected to meet with Lewis and his friends as soon as he returned from the Pro Bowl.

"The devil is busy, always after God's children. He is always trying to get you one way or another," Lewis said when asked about the incidents.

Asked whether he was concerned about his friends and his relationship with the Ravens, Lewis said, "It is something I will discuss with them but not something I can talk about now."

Lewis, 6 feet 1 and 240 pounds, is considered by many to be the best middle linebacker in pro football. He has led the Ravens in tackles since joining the team as a first-round draft pick in 1996. He finished with 198 last year, which might have been his best season with the team.

On Nov. 19, 1998, Modell made Lewis the highest-paid Raven and the highest-paid linebacker with a four-year contract worth $26 million, including a $7 million signing bonus. ∎

Putting trial in past, Lewis says football is now his No. 1 priority

BY JAMISON HENSLEY · JUNE 10, 2000 · THE BALTIMORE SUN

Answering questions from the media for the first time since being cleared of murder charges, a combative Ray Lewis spoke at the Ravens' Owings Mills complex for nearly 17 minutes yesterday. The All-Pro middle linebacker expressed his anger toward Atlanta prosecutors, his fire to return to football and his wish for closure.

"I'm ready to put this behind me," said Lewis, who tapped his right foot repeatedly on the podium. "This is done. This is a chapter that needs to be closed. After this is over, I'm ready to walk away from this."

Lewis, who did not have a prepared statement, said he was exhausted and made a quick exit to his Worthington Valley home immediately after speaking.

Lewis had been on trial in the stabbing deaths of two men in a street brawl Jan. 31 after the Super Bowl in Atlanta. Murder and assault charges were dropped, and Lewis pleaded guilty to obstruction of justice Monday. He testified against his former co-defendants Tuesday.

Yesterday, Lewis acknowledged lying to police during the investigation but said he holds a grudge against Fulton County District Attorney Paul Howard, who brought the murder charges against him.

"Yes, I'm angry at Paul Howard," Lewis said. "Because from day one, I tried to speak to him and tell him that I was an innocent man.

"It's a feeling that I don't think I can express. I would never wish this on my worst enemy to go through what I've been through."

A minute before yesterday's news conference, Lewis' lead defense attorney, Ed Garland, tapped him on the leg and whispered, "This is the day you've been waiting for."

Later, Garland equated Lewis' misdemeanor to a speeding ticket.

"Ray Lewis was totally exonerated," Garland said.

Dressed in a vibrant yellow and brown shirt, khaki pants and sandals, Lewis seemed eager to return to the Ravens and said he expects to work out Monday, when the team begins its four-day veterans camp.

The leading tackler in the NFL last season, he has missed a minicamp and two passing camps this spring.

"Where am I going from here?" Lewis said. "Back to what I've been doing, playing football and enjoying what I do, showing kids that there's still a passion for the game even though you're falsely accused about certain things."

Asked whether the events of the past four months would affect his focus for the season, Lewis cracked a smile for the first time in front of the crowded room.

"I think I'll be more [ticked] off to hit somebody," Lewis said.

Lewis then shrugged off the suggestion that opposing players might use his arrest as ammunition for on-field trash-talking.

"Honestly, I think it'll take a person that's heartless to bring this up in a conversation on the football field," Lewis said. "Regardless of what Ray Lewis does on the football field, two people are dead."

Lewis runs through a drill in training camp in August 2006. He has always found refuge on the field, doing "what I've been doing, playing football and enjoying what I do." *AP Photo*

Ravens owner Art Modell and coach Brian Billick also made statements, supporting Lewis and declaring this subject off limits in the future. Billick, however, said he will continue to address his players about the issue.

The NFL decided Monday not to suspend Lewis but has not determined whether it will fine the 25-year-old player under its player conduct policy.

"We had a great deal of faith in Ray Lewis and that's been borne out, obviously," Billick said. "From this point on, today is the last time we'll discuss this. It is time to move on."

But yesterday, Lewis answered the tough questions, saying he never thought his freedom or his football career was in jeopardy. He said he did not turn his back on Joseph Sweeting and Reginald Oakley, his former co-defendants.

"Did I really turn against them, or did I just tell the truth?" Lewis said.

"To turn against somebody is having involvement in something and then turn your back on it to get yourself out of it. I never did anything. All I did was go up on the stand and told the truth."

When asked why he left two men for dead and did not call police, he said: "There's a lot of things that we don't immediately do. Like I said, you're in situations that you've never been in your life, so you just react. And when you react, your reactions are not all the time right."

So, would Lewis react differently if he could do it again?

"I can't tell you," Lewis said.

Does he think he did anything wrong in lying to the police?

"I think what I did wrong," Lewis said, "I'm paying for now with 12 months of probation.

"I've faced fourth-down-and-1 a lot of times and, you know, I have guys who know that I'm gonna step up in that position. But when it's fourth-down-and-life, you don't know what to do in that situation. And that's what happened when the police approached me and I gave a false statement to them. When you're dealing with fourth-and-life, you never know what you're going to do. I'm angry, I'm mad at myself for the situation I put my family in. I take all responsibility for that."

Lewis said he learned some life-altering lessons after two weeks in jail and two weeks on trial for murder.

"If there's anything I'll change in my lifestyle, it's the choices I make," he said.

"I've always been a guy who's made great choices. Everybody stumbles every once in a while, but I don't think it's about stumbling. It's about recovering, to see where you go from there." ∎

▶Lewis (left) runs with tight end Shannon Sharpe at the end of morning practice in July 2000. *AP Photo*

THE FIRST SUPER BOWL CHAMPIONSHIP

Lewis gets the crowd going during introductions before the Ravens' home opener in September 2000, a 39-36 victory over the Jaguars. *Lloyd Fox | Baltimore Sun Photo*

After difficult year, Lewis voted NFL's top defensive player

BY JAMISON HENSLEY · JANUARY 3, 2001 · THE BALTIMORE SUN

After enduring the most difficult time in his life, Ray Lewis delivered the NFL's most devastating defensive effort this season.

The Ravens' All-Pro middle linebacker was rewarded for his dominant play by winning the Associated Press Defensive Player of the Year award yesterday.

The core of the Ravens' record-setting defense, Lewis was the runaway winner, receiving 30 of the 50 votes from the nationwide panel of sportswriters and broadcasters.

"This is a tremendous honor that I worked my butt off for, and it's finally here," said Lewis, the first Raven to win the award. "A lot of people probably had mixed emotions in the voting. There were some who probably thought I didn't deserve it because of the situation during the offseason. But the people who really know me, and really know football and what I did on the field, those were the people who voted for me."

Lewis, 25, has seen his world come full circle in less than a year.

Last January, he was accused of a double murder in Atlanta after a post-Super Bowl party and spent 16 days in jail. In exchange to pleading guilty to obstructing the police investigation, Lewis was cleared of the murder charges in June and was sentenced to 12 months' probation. Later, he was fined $250,000 by NFL commissioner Paul Tagliabue under the Player Conduct Policy.

But instead of succumbing to the critics off the field and frequent hecklers on the field, Lewis raised his game above his All-Pro level from the previous year. He has also been named the AFC's starting middle linebacker for this year's Pro Bowl, his fourth straight selection.

His presence set the tone for a defense that established NFL records for fewest points (165) and fewest rushing yards (970) allowed in a 16-game season. He led the Ravens in tackles (184) for the fifth straight season and was an all-around force with three sacks, two interceptions, eight pass deflections and three fumble recoveries.

Asked whether this award would silence critics who said he wouldn't be the same after his offseason ordeal, Lewis said: "They were wrong. Anyone who said that now knows it had no effect on me whatsoever." ∎

Baltimore Sun reporter Mike Preston contributed to this article.

►Lewis reacts after making a play against the Jaguars in September 2000, the Ravens' second victory in a row en route to a 5-1 start. The team lost three straight after that, then reeled off 11 consecutive victories, the last being Super Bowl XXXV. *Karl Merton Ferron | Baltimore Sun Photo*

Purple reign: Lewis, Ravens defense back up boasts, silence Giants in Super Bowl, 34-7

BY KEN MURRAY · JANUARY 29, 2001 · THE BALTIMORE SUN

Now there can be no doubt.
The Ravens claimed their place in history last night with one final dissertation on great defense.

A team that swaggered into Super Bowl XXXV delivered on its sound and fury of the past week with a 34-7 demolition of the New York Giants before 71,921 at Raymond James Stadium in Tampa, Fla.

It was the crowning glory, and defining moment, of a season that produced Baltimore's first Super Bowl championship in 30 years, since the Colts beat the Dallas Cowboys, 16-13, in Super Bowl V in 1971.

Collecting four interceptions against overmatched quarterback Kerry Collins, the wild-card Ravens (16-4) completed the improbable turnaround from perennial loser to Super Bowl champion in only coach Brian Billick's second season.

Their 11th straight victory followed a formula that proved unbeatable down the stretch: suffocating defense, opportunistic special teams and a timely play on offense.

They got a 38-yard touchdown pass from quarterback Trent Dilfer to Brandon Stokley for the early lead, an 84-yard kickoff return for a clinching touchdown, and an MVP performance from team leader and middle linebacker Ray Lewis.

Lewis had five tackles and deflected four passes to become the seventh defensive player in the history of the Super Bowl – and first middle linebacker – to win the Pete Rozelle Award as MVP.

"It was amazing the way we came out," Lewis said. "I mean, it was incredible to see the way we came out and played as a team. This defense has been doing this all year, and never, never got the credit.

"This win is something they can't take away from us. We are the best ever, the best ever right now."

The triumph completed Lewis' journey back from infamy. After last season's Super Bowl in Atlanta, he was charged in a double murder and had to undergo a high-profile trial. Even after the charges were dropped in a plea bargain agreement in exchange for an obstruction of justice misdemeanor charge, Lewis had the cloud of suspicion over him.

Yesterday, Lewis dominated play in the first half when the Ravens grabbed a 10-0 lead they would not relinquish.

"He has a way of always setting the tone," said defensive coordinator Marvin Lewis. "He sets the tone when he comes out of that tunnel. He's been that way from the very first day he walked into that building. He's set the tone for this organization. He's a quality person, a quality player, and you see everyone feed off of it."

The Ravens defense backed up a week of bravado that had several players calling for a shutout and their rightful place among the best defenses in NFL history.

The Ravens didn't get the shutout – New York's Ron Dixon returned a kickoff for a 97-yard touchdown in the third quarter – even though they deserved one.

Lewis, who had three solo tackles, assisted on two tackles and deflected four passes, brings down Giants tight end Howard Cross during Super Bowl XXXV in January 2001. The Ravens held New York to 33 second-half yards. *AP Photo*

Baltimore's defense allowed the Giants just 33 total yards in the second half, and 152 for the game. The Giants were only 2-for-14 on third down.

In their four-game Super Bowl run, the Ravens defense gave up just one touchdown, and the team outscored its opponents by a combined 95-23.

"This is the best defense ever to play the game," defensive tackle Tony Siragusa said. ∎

Lewis' whirlwind year culminates with MVP in sport's ultimate game

BY JAMISON HENSLEY · JANUARY 29, 2001 · THE BALTIMORE SUN

After a week of being interrogated about his past, Ray Lewis answered with the definitive performance of Super Bowl XXXV as the Ravens routed the New York Giants, 34-7, at Raymond James Stadium in Tampa, Fla.

The Ravens' All-Pro middle linebacker continued to climb the echelon of the all-time greats at his position, spearheading one of the most stifling defensive performances in the sport's ultimate game.

From the moment he danced onto the field in introductions, Lewis proved to be the commanding presence and became just the seventh defensive player to win the Super Bowl Most Valuable Player award.

It has been a whirlwind experience for Lewis.

Last year, he was charged, along with two companions, in the stabbing deaths of two men in a post-Super Bowl street brawl in Atlanta on Jan. 31.

Now, he stands at the pinnacle of his career.

"The thing is, the man upstairs tells you I never would take you through hell without bringing you through triumph," said Lewis, with a smile fixed upon his face.

"That's why I'm sitting up here now."

Lewis, who eventually pleaded guilty to obstruction of justice and received 12 months'

Lewis is congratulated by NFL commissioner Paul Tagliabue during a news conference the day after the Super Bowl. "The man upstairs tells you I never would take you through hell without bringing you through triumph," Lewis told reporters. *AP Photo*

probation, was besieged by hundreds of reporters all week about the incident. He was criticized by the national media for not showing remorse.

The Ravens saw the irony in the game's most vilified player finishing as its hero.

"It's only fitting," tight end Shannon Sharpe said. "You might not like some of the things he's said or you might not like the person that he is, but you can't argue with his talent. The guy is the best

Lewis became the center of attention during Super Bowl week as he was asked to address questions from a throng of media concerning his decision to plead guilty to obstruction of justice in a double-murder trial in Atlanta. Reporters criticized him for not showing remorse. *Karl Merton Ferron | Baltimore Sun Photo*

player in football right now. But the scary thing is that he's only 25 years old."

The NFL's Defensive Player of the Year chimed in with his rebuttal for all those critics.

"If they're waiting [for] me to stumble now," Lewis began, "I'll just stumble with a ring on."

Lewis' impact extended beyond his statistics. He was credited with five tackles, tying his season low.

The centerpiece of the Ravens' record-setting defense established the relentless tone early. In the first quarter, the Giants couldn't avoid Lewis, who deflected two passes and made three tackles.

But when the Ravens became the third defense not to surrender points in the Super Bowl (with the Miami Dolphins in 1973 and Pittsburgh Steelers in 1975), the lasting image was the impenetrable Lewis.

"There is no feeling like this right now," Lewis said. "If I could express it, it wouldn't be a true feeling. My body is tingling right now."

Still, was Lewis upset the special teams allowed the 97-yard kickoff return by Ron Dixon in the third quarter that shattered the defense's campaign for a shutout?

"It hurt," he said. "But our defense knows that they didn't score any points."

Lewis is soaking in the moment, escaping tragedy to make history.

For Lewis, he answered the critics. And he did it in a dominant fashion.

"If you put it in a storybook," Lewis said, "nobody would believe it." ∎

After trial, Lewis became leader, took out fury on field

BY MIKE KLINGAMAN · OCTOBER 22, 2010 · THE BALTIMORE SUN

Ray Lewis peered out at the roomful of Ravens waiting to hear from their embattled team leader. A pep talk it would not be.

On Jan. 31, 2000, Lewis was charged with murder in the stabbing deaths of two men in Atlanta. Now, about half a year later, the All-Pro linebacker stood before teammates at training camp in Westminster, knowing that what he said could pull the Ravens together – or push them apart.

Lewis hadn't planned to address the Ravens that day. A friend, Hall of Famer Jim Brown, was in town and had agreed to speak to the players. But when he rose to do so, Brown surprised them all.

"There are many things I can say to you guys today, but I don't think you need to hear from me," Brown told them. "You need to hear from your leader."

Brown sat down. Lewis, then 25, stood up – and held nothing back.

"He put everything out in the open," quarterback Trent Dilfer said.

"Instead of sweeping [the incident] under the rug and having it be the pink elephant in the room, Ray said, 'Here's what's going on, and how I'm dealing with it.'"

Lewis' animated talk lasted 10 minutes, players said.

"He wasn't subdued," safety Kim Herring recalled. "At the end, we all said, 'All right, cool – now let's move forward.'"

Thus began the season that would culminate in a Ravens Super Bowl title and catapult Lewis into the upper echelon of NFL players. To that point,

he had been a prodigious talent. That day he transformed into a leader, and he remains one of the most revered motivators in sports.

Lewis had acted irresponsibly on the night of the tragedy, advising those he was with not to speak to police. The NFL fined him $250,000 for violating its conduct policy, and in some ways his tarnish spread to the rest of the Ravens. Most of his teammates, though, were able to take an uncomplicated view of the situation: The judicial system had spoken, and Lewis was an innocent man trudging through unwarranted character assassination.

By speaking so frankly on the first day they were gathered as a team, Lewis made clear the way he planned to act that year. As with any championship run, a thousand things – from finding the right quarterback to having a few fumbles bounce the right way – had to happen, but if there was a force that gave the team an identity, it was Lewis.

"What he said that day cast a vision for us," kicker Matt Stover said.

"Basically, he said, 'Follow me,' and we did. It gave us a spark, a trust, a bond that turned something so horribly terrifying and life-changing into such a positive for the team."

Lewis was preaching to the choir.

"We all knew what Ray was accused of was false," defensive end Rob Burnett said. Mahatma "Gandhi could have talked to the team that day, and it wouldn't have changed our minds about the character of Ray Lewis."

Publicly, however, the issue festered. Whenever

Lewis, right, greets legendary Browns running back Jim Brown during a practice before Super Bowl XXXV. Half a year earlier, Brown thought Ravens players needed to hear from Lewis about his role in what happened in Atlanta the previous January. *AP Photo*

the club hit the road, fans targeted Lewis, called him a killer and picketed the places where the team stayed.

"Signs, you can ignore," Burnett said. "But when people have the luxury of seats close to our bench, it gives them a soapbox from which to spit venom.

The things that came out of their mouths made me want to jump up in the stands and do things that my parents didn't raise me to do."

Now, Lewis acknowledges the threats on his life were so real that he checked into out-of-town hotels under an assumed name. Yet in spite of the danger – or, perhaps, because of it – he played that season with an unprecedented focus and ferocity leading the Ravens to 11 straight victories and an NFL championship.

With all of the hubbub swirling around Lewis off the field, football became his sanctuary, teammates said.

"Ray went out and exerted his anger toward opponents on the field," linebacker Cornell Brown said. "He found he could release that pain outside of him – the things you can't say out loud, but you can say in a hit."

Lewis agreed.

"Yeah, yeah, that's it," he said of his stepped-up intensity in 2000. "If I wouldn't have went through all that [in Atlanta], maybe I wouldn't have had the year that I had."

Had the tragedy not occurred, "I don't think that we'd have gone to the Super Bowl," guard Edwin Mulitalo said. "Ray was great before that, but that incident gave him extra focus and pushed us over the top."

In turn, Lewis raised the bar for the team, which rallied around him, Mulitalo said.

"Ray was our cornerstone, and we fed off of him," he said. "Not only did we circle the wagons [around Lewis], we were bumper to bumper."

Added Dilfer: "It was a concerted effort each week to rally around our brother. There were times, in Pittsburgh, Cleveland and Tennessee, when, getting off the team bus, a bunch of us wanted to get into fights" with fans maligning Lewis. "You had to control your emotions a lot. It was a test, all year long."

Ravens coach Brian Billick milked the us-versus-them situation for all it was worth, Dilfer said.

"Ray's case fueled the bunker mentality that we rallied behind every week," Dilfer said. "Billick made sure we had a chip on our shoulder all year."

In a recent interview with Baltimore Sun columnist Peter Schmuck, Billick recalled the way the story followed the team. Media covering opposing teams would write about it each week.

"So you dredge it all up again," he said. "And you walk out in the stadium behind Ray and you hear some of the things people – idiots – can say, and it does galvanize you. That 'us against them' was very, very real."

Making Lewis the poster boy for the 2000 Ravens was a gutsy move on the coach's part, players said.

"What if Ray had done something else wrong [off the field]?" Brown said.

"It would have looked bad for Billick, standing up for this guy. It definitely could have backfired on the coach."

Fans tried to rile the middle linebacker. Rod Woodson recalled a preseason game at Washington in which signs were brought into

▶Lewis, pictured in August 2001, said in 2010 of the slayings, "No day leaves this Earth without me asking God to ease the pain of anybody who was affected by that whole ordeal." *John Makely. | Baltimore Sun Photo*

the stadium, including one that read, "Ray Lewis, killer of sons."

"I was livid," said Woodson, a Hall of Fame defensive back. "Ray had to hold me back. But, you know, in a weird way, it kind of made us all closer. We all started going bowling on Thursday nights to get away from everything. It made us more like family than a football team."

Nationally, it wasn't a feel-good title run. Lewis' transgressions led the media to vilify the team in newspapers from The (Bergen, N.J.) Record ("The Ravens are a polluted parade of bad acts") to The Miami Herald ("Satan's favorite team won the Super Bowl").

The day he learned he had won NFL Defensive Player of the Year, Lewis was assailed on the air by Don Imus, the radio talk show host, who said he would root against Baltimore in the playoffs because it harbored "a murderer."

The Ravens won anyway, and Lewis was named Most Valuable Player of the 34-7 victory over the New York Giants.

Never mind that in the aftermath he was spurned as the "I'm going to Disney World" pitchman. Or that General Mills snubbed Lewis and put the faces of five other Ravens on its Super Bowl commemorative Wheaties box.

The year that began so horrifically ended with accolades.

"That [championship] was the diamond that came out of the coal," Mulitalo said. "But it would have been nice if it had happened some other way."

A rare look into the past

In the 10 years since that Super Bowl, Lewis has cemented his place as one of the league's all-time top linebackers. Though the incident in Atlanta will always be part of his life, it is seldom mentioned anymore.

Lewis, who has gone on to become a commercial pitchman and iconic figure in Baltimore, has rarely discussed what happened in Atlanta, or how those events changed him. But in a recent interview with The Sun, he shared his thoughts on that turbulent year and how it shaped his life.

"I'm telling you, no day leaves this Earth without me asking God to ease the pain of anybody who was affected by that whole ordeal," he said of the slayings. "He's a God who tests people – not that he put me in that situation, because he

didn't make me go nowhere. I put myself in that situation.

"But if I had to go through all of that over again ... I wouldn't change a thing. Couldn't. The end result is who I am now."

Lewis said he tried to tune out the fans' vitriolic taunts.

"I've never stopped carrying that on my shoulders," he said. "During that year, I said, 'You know what? Whatever people are going to say, they're going to say.'

"The sad part is, you hear the ignorance of the way people speak about something they have no clue about. So when you do hear those things, you start to pray for people like that. [Even now] when I'm in opposing stadiums, I just recite our Father's prayer to calm my mind down."

'It probably saved his life'

Lewis coped, knowing the Ravens had his back, on the field and off.

"From all the crazy things going on in those stadiums, from the signs to the words people were saying, [his teammates] were right there," he said. "It defines what brotherhood means and why we're put here, so that one day, if you find yourself [in a jam], you've got somebody worthy enough to talk to."

All season, Lewis played with "the passion of a warrior," Stover said, especially on the road. He had 13 tackles (12 unassisted) and received a game ball in a 15-10 victory at Jacksonville. In a one-point win at Tennessee, Lewis leveled Eddie George, the Titans' star running back, with a crushing hit in the first half that demoralized George for the rest of the game. And in the divisional round of the playoffs, Lewis intercepted a Tennessee pass and raced 50 yards for a touchdown to seal the Ravens' 24-10 victory.

Meanwhile, in the aftermath of Atlanta, players sensed a maturity not seen before in Lewis.

"He totally became a man that year," Brown said. "The time he spent in jail, alone, gave Ray a lot of time to check himself."

Lional Dalton, a defensive tackle, said Lewis "went from being childish off the field to more of a leader. He hung out with more positive people, and he kept his circle tight."

"It probably saved his life."

Woodson agreed.

"That [incident] slapped Ray into reality," he

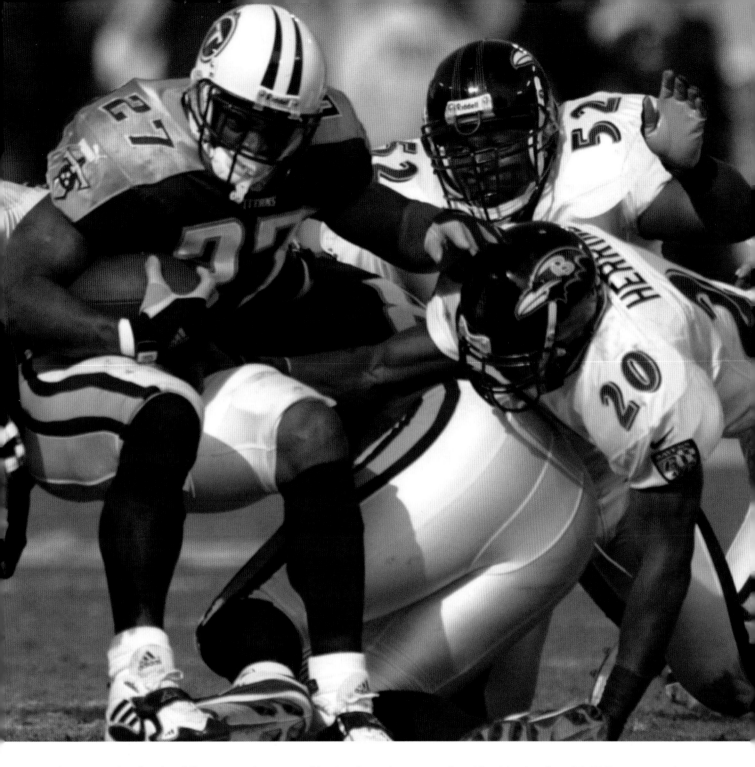

Titans running back Eddie George is stopped by Lewis and strong safety Kim Herring in a 24-23 Ravens road win in November 2000. Lewis leveled George with a vicious hit during the game. *Doug Kapustin | Baltimore Sun Photo*

said. "I don't know if he'd be the player he is today if he hadn't gone through that. It made him appreciate what he had on the field. He'd always been a tackling machine, but that year he became a playmaker, a leader.

"It was unfortunate that it had to happen that way, but we all have a different journey."

But it was a fitting theme for the team that year, Mulitalo said.

"Every Super Bowl team has its story, and this just happens to be ours. In a weird, ironic way, how else would it be for the Ravens?" ∎

GREATNESS AFFIRMED IN MIDCAREER

Lewis jokes with the media in August 2002 after signing a seven-year contract with the Ravens worth about $50 million that includes an NFL-record signing bonus of $19 million. "I truly believe they respect what I did and what I'm still able to do for this organization," he said. *Lloyd Fox | Baltimore Sun Photo*

Lewis signs 7-year contract with record $19 million bonus

BY JAMISON HENSLEY · AUGUST 2, 2002 · THE BALTIMORE SUN

Ray Lewis made NFL history again. The Ravens' All-Pro linebacker delivered the finishing blow to five months of negotiations, calling his agent at 12:30 yesterday morning and ordering him to seal the deal. Less than 12 hours later, Lewis was signing a seven-year contract worth about $50 million that includes an NFL-record signing bonus of $19 million.

Lewis' bonus represents the largest up-front, no-option payment in league history, surpassing the $16 million given to Ravens left tackle Jonathan Ogden before the 2000 season. It continued the trend of escalating salaries in sports, following baseball's Alex Rodriguez (10 years, $252 million) and basketball's Shaquille O'Neal (three years, $88.4 million).

"I truly believe they respect what I did and what I'm still able to do for this organization," said Lewis, the NFL's Defensive Player of the Year in 2000 and the Most Valuable Player of Super Bowl XXXV.

Minutes after signing the whopping deal, Lewis resembled a kid on Christmas morning rather than the most-feared linebacker in the NFL.

He talked about breaking down into tears while calling his mother to tell her that she was financially set for life. It wasn't so long ago when Lewis earned money by cutting lawns for $10 a day.

"I'm a country boy," said Lewis, 27, who grew up in Lakeland, Fla. "So this is cool."

Lewis' record-setting deal ended dragged-out talks that featured three face-to-face meetings in three different states, 12 faxed proposals, an impromptu conversation in a parking lot and a verbal sparring match between Ravens coach Brian Billick and agent Roosevelt Barnes.

In the end, an agreement was reached by a late call from Lewis and some compromising.

According to a league source, the Ravens were offering a signing bonus of $18 million while Lewis' agent was asking for $21 million. The sides decided to find a common ground on the contract, which is believed to include guaranteed money through 2005.

When asked to sum up the negotiations, Lewis glanced over each shoulder to make certain there were no team officials around.

Then, flashing a big smile, he whispered, "I won. I got what I wanted."

The Ravens got what they wanted as well, locking up Lewis for several years while gaining between $1 million to $1.5 million in desperately needed salary cap room.

By signing Lewis yesterday, the Ravens' monumental rebuilding project has its cornerstone.

"I've seen them all play at middle linebacker, Dick Butkus, Ray Nitschke.

... But the greatest by far is Ray Lewis," Ravens owner Art Modell said. "And I predict a great future." ■

► Ravens trainer Bill Tessendorf checks the range of motion on Lewis' left shoulder in December 2002, a week after surgery to repair a torn labrum that sidelined him for 11 games. *John Makely | Baltimore Sun Photo*

Ray, Jamal Lewis capture AP Player of the Year awards

BY BRENT JONES · JANUARY 1, 2004 · THE BALTIMORE SUN

Three days after Jamal Lewis fell short of making NFL history, the Ravens' rugged running back combined with linebacker Ray Lewis to do so yesterday.

The Lewises (who are not related) became the first teammates to win the Associated Press offensive and defensive Player of the Year awards.

Jamal Lewis received 29 of 50 votes by a nationwide panel of sportswriters and broadcasters for Offensive Player of the Year, easily beating San Diego Chargers running back LaDainian Tomlinson, the runner-up with eight votes.

Ray Lewis received 43 of 50 votes, winning the defensive honor for the second time in his eight-year career.

Yesterday's honors come after Jamal Lewis ran for 114 yards in Sunday's regular-season finale, a 13-10 win over the Pittsburgh Steelers, to become the fifth player to top the 2,000-yard rushing mark for a season. Lewis finished with 2,066 rushing yards, the second-highest season total in league history, 39 shy of Eric Dickerson's record.

Ray Lewis also had one of his better games of the season against the Steelers, leading the team with 15 tackles and an interception. He set a Ravens record with 225 tackles this season.

"The beauty of it is, that's what we set out to do at the beginning of this year," Ray Lewis said of the awards.

Ernie Accorsi, general manager of the New York Giants, expressed admiration for both Lewises.

"Ray Lewis is simply the best defensive player in the league and one of the greatest linebackers I have seen in 54 years of watching the NFL," Accorsi said. "And Jamal Lewis just warms the hearts of those of us who love the big back. One thing will never change. ... You still don't want to tackle the big, fast guy who hurts you.

"Both players are examples of why no club in this league does a better job in player personnel than Baltimore."

For Ray Lewis, this year was as much about redemption as it was dominance.

Last year, he separated his left shoulder and eventually needed season-ending surgery. During what might have been the best year of his career, he hurt the shoulder in the fourth game, against the Cleveland Browns, and played just once more the rest of the season.

Vowing to come back better than ever, Lewis set career highs this year in solo tackles (160), interceptions (six) and forced fumbles (two).

"We said that if me and Jamal are healthy, we have a great chance of going back to the Super Bowl," Lewis said. "Once again, we're healthy. It's hard to walk into a game and game plan against both of us. You have to deal with Jamal, who can run all day, and then deal with me, who can talk all day. One way or another, you'll have to deal with one Lewis. It's a great one-two tandem that we have." ∎

Baltimore Sun reporter Ken Murray contributed to this article.

Jamal Lewis, left, was named 2003 Associated Press Offensive Player of the Year after rushing for 2,066 yards, second most in NFL history. Ray Lewis was selected Defensive Player of the Year after making 160 solo tackles and six interceptions and forcing two fumbles.   *Gene Sweeney, Jr. | Baltimore Sun Photo*

Pulling down college degree is Lewis' proudest tackle

BY MIKE PRESTON · MAY 9, 2004 · THE BALTIMORE SUN

Ravens inside linebacker Ray Lewis has won the Super Bowl Most Valuable Player and been honored as the NFL's Defensive Player of the Year, but his greatest achievement might come Saturday when he walks across a stage on the University of Maryland campus.

Nearly eight years after he left the University of Miami as a junior to enter the NFL draft, and on the day of his 29th birthday, Lewis will earn a bachelor of arts degree from Maryland in business administration.

Talk about euphoria. To Lewis, this is better than taking out Eddie George and Steve McNair in a playoff game, or earning a sixth consecutive Pro Bowl appearance. Lewis will have a cheering section of 45 close friends and family members at graduation.

"This is better than those awards. This is an idea you start with as a child, and no one can take it from you," Lewis said. "You really don't know if you can be a Most Valuable Player, but this is something you can achieve if you make up your mind and think about going as high as you can."

Lewis, a business law major at Miami, had promised his mother, Sunseria, that he would return to get the final 24 credits needed to graduate shortly before he announced he was going pro. He took classes online and on campus during the offseasons.

We've all heard stories about athletes who said they were going to return to graduate, only to obtain fame and fortune, and throw out the idea as quickly as Major League Baseball ditched putting the "Spider-Man 2" movie logo on the bases.

It's a sad commentary, especially when the stardom subsides and the athletes have nothing to rely on. But Lewis is impressive. He earned his degree while in the prime of his career. He is unquestionably the best defensive player in the league and has tons of money and fame.

And now he will have a college degree.

For Lewis, there was never any doubt about going back. He is the first of one brother and three sisters to earn a college degree.

"Back at Miami, I had like a 3.2 grade-point average until I started leaving and began preparing for football," Lewis said. "It was always important to me, and I told my mom I was going to go back and get it.

"Actually, she just found out about the graduation when she saw the bill for my cap and gown," Lewis said. "This is special for her and me." ■

▶Lewis pumps up the fans before a 20-14 home win against the Browns. Lewis made a different kind of entrance seven years earlier, walking across a stage to receive his college degree at Maryland.
Gene Sweeney, Jr. | Baltimore Sun Photo

Lewis to sign 3-year deal, keeping him here from start to finish

BY MIKE PRESTON · MARCH 5, 2009 · THE BALTIMORE SUN

The prodigal son has returned to Baltimore.

After failing to find a fortune in other areas of the country, linebacker Ray Lewis, one of Baltimore's all-time favorite sports figures, agreed in principle to a reported three-year, incentive-laden contract worth $22 million with the Ravens.

Now Lewis can finish his Hall of Fame career in Baltimore and this city's love affair with No. 52 can continue after a brief separation.

Oh, Lewis' image has lost some luster in the community that it will never regain, but not on the field. Over the weekend, a lot of Ravens fans swore off Lewis. Some of us laughed when he didn't get the big free-agent contract or even a phone call from one other team. A lot of us didn't care one way or the other.

But now that he's back, Baltimore fans will love Lewis again. The anger at his words about playing for another team might not subside until training camp, but all of it will end at the introductions at the season opener.

Lewis will be announced, and once he comes out and does that ugly "Squirrel" dance, all will be forgiven. And as soon as he pounds on his chest after making a tackle or sticks his tongue out while on the video board, the entire stadium will erupt.

Welcome back, Ray-Ray.

Baltimore fans have a special place in their hearts for their sports heroes. Johnny Unitas once left Baltimore for San Diego, but no one ever held that against him. Former Oriole Eddie Murray left on bad terms but draws a rousing reception every time he returns here. Regardless of what Lewis has said during free agency, he has always embodied what this town is about. He was once an undersized, underrated middle linebacker who came out of the University of Miami, and he has made a name for himself by playing as hard as he can all the time and with a chip on his shoulder.

Lewis' blue-collar work ethic on the field is so Baltimore.

He hurt a lot of fans with his talk about possibly playing for the Dallas Cowboys and the New York Jets. One of Lewis' major mistakes throughout his career is surrounding himself with yes men, people who tell him exactly what he wants to hear. His agent, David Dunn, should be fired for the way he handled these negotiations, because it was Dunn who planted in Lewis' head that he could demand a Peyton Manning-type contract at age 33.

It was Dunn who should have been the mouthpiece during these negotiations, not Lewis mouthing off at some pool in Honolulu at the Pro Bowl. It was a total

►Lewis celebrates after shooting a gap between center and right guard to crush running back Darren Sproles for a 5-yard loss on fourth-and-2 from the Ravens 15-yard line in the final seconds of a 31-26 win against the Chargers in September 2009 in San Diego. "He made the greatest play I've ever seen," Ravens coach John Harbaugh said.
Karl Merton Ferron | Baltimore Sun Photo

embarrassment then, and again last week when Lewis didn't receive an offer.

Regardless, Lewis is back as a Raven. We would have all adjusted to his playing in a new uniform next season, but now we don't have to. For at least another year or two, we get to see him dancing during warmups. We get to see him pile-driving a few more running backs and tight ends into the turf. We get to see him signing autographs in training camp long after the other players have gone into the locker room.

There can be no other No. 52 in Baltimore history. He revolutionized his position and won the Ravens a Super Bowl. And now, in his twilight years, he gets to finish out his career in Baltimore, where he will become an iconic figure before he gets a bust in Canton, Ohio.

The professional career of Ray Lewis is ending in the right place. There is no better city than Baltimore, where it began. He ticked off all of us in recent weeks, but we'll put that behind us. Welcome back, No. 52. ■

►Coach John Harbaugh, left, and Lewis share a light moment during a media session at a minicamp in May 2009 in Owings Mills. Lewis played his final five NFL seasons under Harbaugh despite threatening to leave the team in free agency during the 2009 offseason. *Karl Merton Ferron | Baltimore Sun Photo*

'Big Play Ray' is the gift that keeps on giving

BY JAMISON HENSLEY · NOVEMBER 28, 2010 · THE BALTIMORE SUN

Ray Lewis always tries to give back, whether it's to the Ravens or the city of Baltimore.

Two days after sealing a Ravens victory with another big play, the magnetizing middle linebacker was making an impact in a different way in West Baltimore, where he handed out 800 turkeys to needy families.

A Thanksgiving tradition over the past 11 years, Lewis has provided food, handshakes and hugs to the people of his adopted hometown.

From Lewis' perspective, it's not about handouts. It's about being hands-on.

"I was once in that line before," Lewis said. "Me and my mom, we grew up hard. She made sure that when we got older, we knew that giving back was one of the most important things."

There will be a time when Lewis will leave the football field. But he says he'll never leave Baltimore.

"I got a true vision to clean up Baltimore," he said. "I want us to go away from being rated the No. 2 murder capital of the world and become a place where people are comfortable coming here and not worry about this craziness."

Lewis, who lived in Florida and played college football at Miami, is rooted in the Baltimore community.

He runs the Ray Lewis Foundation, which gives

Lewis gets a hug from Gwendolyn Barnes as he drops a turkey into her food basket in November 2011 at a Thanksgiving giveaway at W. E. B. Du Bois High School in northeast Baltimore. The event was sponsored by the Ray Lewis 52 Foundation, a nonprofit that provides personal and economic assistance to disadvantaged youths.
Gene Sweeney, Jr. | Baltimore Sun Photo

financial help to disadvantaged youth. He has fed more than 4,000 families the past decade at his Thanksgiving event. He held boot camp fitness sessions for Baltimore City police officers and members of a local homeless shelter last year. He's building a bowling lane and entertainment complex at Hunt Valley Towne Centre.

To honor his contributions, the city renamed a section of North Avenue "Ray Lewis Way" six months ago.

"It's a blessing that he has the heart to do all of this for a community," Pamela Johnson said while getting a turkey from Lewis. ■

▲Lewis, in a light brown suit, looks up at the street sign that was unveiled during a ceremony in May 2010. Standing with him are family members and city officials. The North Avenue corridor, at the corner of Broadway, is home to the DIAKON Center, where the Ravens star and his charitable foundation host an annual Thanksgiving distribution for nearly 1,000 Baltimore families in need. *Kim Hairston | Baltimore Sun Photo*

◄Lewis greets London Seldon, 4, as fellow Cherry Hill resident Brandon Coates, 12, smiles in December 2009. Walmart donated turkeys and toys to 200 families from Bethel AME, a church struck by lightning five months earlier. *Lloyd Fox | Baltimore Sun Photo*

At high-impact position, Lewis' longevity sets him apart

BY JAMISON HENSLEY · AUGUST 28, 2011 · THE BALTIMORE SUN

About a month after last season ended, Ravens defensive coordinator Chuck Pagano received a text from a friend that read: "I'm watching one of your players run in the sand for an hour."

Later that morning, another text flashed on Pagano's phone: "Now, I'm watching your player swim 30 minutes in the ocean."

When Pagano finally asked for the name of the player, it was as if he already knew the answer: Ray Lewis.

The enduring face of the franchise is entering his 16th season – a feat impressive for any NFL player, much less an inside linebacker – and the secret of Lewis' longevity is really no secret at all.

The 36-year-old Lewis prides himself on outworking everyone, whether on the field, in film study or in the weight room.

Lewis' 210 games played is fourth most among active players, behind a kicker (Jason Hanson), long snapper (David Binn) and fullback (Tony Richardson). None has been in as many high-impact collisions or logged as many plays as Lewis.

That's why coaches praise him and players look up to him. Even major league baseball's "Iron Man" admires Lewis' durability.

"The fact that Ray has been able to play the game at such a high level for so long is amazing to me," said Cal Ripken Jr., who holds baseball's record for consecutive games played at 2,632. "His passion for football is clear, and I would imagine that it is that love of the game that keeps him going so strong. As a Ravens fan, I have enjoyed watching him play since his career began here in Baltimore."

Just as no one can talk about Orioles history without mentioning Ripken, the same goes for the Ravens and Lewis.

He is the longest-tenured Raven on the roster by six seasons (safety Ed Reed is second). The Ravens selected Lewis in the draft before they selected their team colors.

Lewis rarely misses time because of injury; he has played in 14 or more games in all but two of his 15 seasons.

Lewis closes in on Steelers quarterback Charlie Batch on a third-down play during the third quarter of a 17-14 win in October 2010 in Pittsburgh. Even late in his career, the Ravens would rarely take Lewis off the field, even in obvious passing situations. "It would take a tractor and chain to pull him off," defensive coordinator Chuck Pagano said in 2011. "Because all of those other guys feed off his energy, he raises everyone else's bar." *Karl Merton Ferron. | Baltimore Sun Photo*

He is the team's ultimate survivor, lasting through three head coaches, two salary cap purges (2002 and this year) and one trip into free agency. This year's first-round pick, cornerback Jimmy Smith, was 8 years old when Lewis played his first NFL game.

While few players have lasted as long as Lewis, even fewer have been playing as well at this stage of their careers. Lewis was the highest-rated defensive player in an NFL Network poll of current players, ranking No. 4 overall behind Tom Brady, Peyton Manning and Adrian Peterson.

"He's still playing as well as any middle linebacker in football today," Ravens coach John Harbaugh said. "I want him to play as long as he wants to play, and I think he'll know when it's time. But as he has told me before, it's not time."

Trying to figure out that "time" is as difficult as breaking a Lewis tackle.

He recently said he might retire after this season if the Ravens win the Super Bowl, but he doesn't guarantee it.

"I don't know when it will all be over for me," Lewis told CBS Sports. "People want to use my age against me. They say I'm too old. People fear getting old. I don't fear that because now I have wisdom and a tough body to go with that wisdom."

When Lewis will end his Hall of Fame career has been a hot topic in recent years.

Four months ago, Lewis hinted that he would play two more seasons, telling the NFL Network that he can't see playing football past age 37. His contract runs through 2015.

"People would always ask me about when Ray would retire, and I used to say, 'Next year,' " linebacker Jarret Johnson said. "Now, I don't even say anything. I don't even guess. To me, he could play 25 more years because he comes in every year in better and better and better shape."

No other great middle linebacker has played as long as Lewis.

Mike Singletary retired after 12 seasons with the Chicago Bears before his play declined. The Pittsburgh Steelers' Jack Lambert walked away after 11 years because of a severe toe injury. And the Bears' Dick Butkus stopped after nine seasons because of knee injuries.

One of the reasons Lewis can continue to take the field is how he takes care of his body off it.

His offseason regimen over the years has included kickboxing, martial arts, swimming and wrestling. This past year, he's picked up cycling because it improves cardiovascular conditioning "without all that pounding."

"My world is a violent world," Lewis said. "That's why I train so hard. I don't know if I have ever found a man on this Earth that would flat-out outwork me."

There has been talk within the organization of reducing Lewis' snaps to extend his career. When asked whether the Ravens are thinking about lessening Lewis' workload, Pagano said: "You can't take him out of there. It would take a tractor and chain to pull him off the field. Because all of those other guys feed off his energy, he raises everyone else's bar. They see No. 52 on all of those downs, and it's all about accountability – we're not going to let this guy down." ∎

►Lewis returns an interception thrown by Jeff Garcia 29 yards for a touchdown during the second quarter of the Ravens' 44-6 home rout of the 49ers. Lewis is the only NFL player with at least 40 sacks and 30 interceptions; this is one of three regular-season picks he took to the end zone during his career.
Doug Kapustin | Baltimore Sun Photo

Lewis ranked No. 5 on Baltimore Sun's top 175 athletes of past 175 years

BY **MIKE KLINGAMAN** · MAY 13, 2012 · THE BALTIMORE SUN

Ray Lewis is the oldest Raven – he turns 37 on Tuesday – but as one of The Baltimore Sun's top 10 all-time Maryland athletes, he's just a kid. Eight of his peers are Hall of Famers in their respective sports. Seven were stars before Lewis was born.

The breadth of their accomplishments is not lost on the Ravens linebacker.

"Look at the guys on that list, [Johnny] Unitas and Brooks [Robinson], and the impact they had. They were staples in this city, known as much for what they did off the field as on it," Lewis said. "When I look at the history here, with Babe [Ruth] and Cal [Ripken], I think, 'Wow.' For me to come under that umbrella shows that people believe in me.

"And I'm No. 5? That's a good number. It's honorable just to be there."

Statistics bear him out. Twice the NFL Defensive Player of the Year (2000 and 2003), Lewis is a 13-time Pro Bowl selection and a seven-time first-team All-Pro. He was voted Most Valuable Player of the January 2001 Super Bowl. Beforehand, he crowed, "Give us 10 points and the game is over." The Ravens crushed the New York Giants, 34-7.

The league's leading tackler among active players (2,586), Lewis has 40.5 career sacks and 31 interceptions in a 16-year career.

It's not the future he expected as a first-round draft pick in 1996.

"I was taken [26th overall] by a team that didn't even exist yet, that had no identity," he said. "I'm thinking, 'What's going on?' "

Now, Lewis said, "I could never imagine playing nowhere else. No disrespect to other cities, but wherever we go, I can't see myself there.

"No matter where I go across this world, somebody sees me and says, 'Baltimore' – and that's a blessing. I brought a winning energy here. I think, when I was a baby, God must've said, 'I got a city waiting for you, a place where you'll change lives and give hope back to people.' "

Retirement – and the obligatory five-year wait to enter the Pro Football Hall of Fame – is not yet in the offing, Lewis said.

"I can't walk away when I'm lovin' what I do and doin' it the way that I am," he said. "I'm going to get all I can out of me. I came into this game to give it all I got – and then I'll hang up my cleats.

"There's nothing I haven't accomplished that I wanted to do, on the field or off. For me to have walked my son into the University of Miami [Lewis' alma mater] with a scholarship was the last thing on my bucket list."

When he's gone, Lewis said, make his a simple epitaph.

"All I want is those famous two words: 'Well done.' " ∎

▸Lewis smiles on the last day of training camp in 2010. In The Baltimore Sun's 2012 ranking of the top 175 Maryland athletes of the past 175 years, he finished behind Babe Ruth, Johnny Unitas, Brooks Robinson and Frank Robinson. Lewis was followed in the top 10 by Cal Ripken Jr., Michael Phelps, Jimmie Foxx, Jim Parker and Wes Unseld. *Lloyd Fox. | Baltimore Sun Photo*

GOING OUT AS A CHAMPION

Lewis displays the Vince Lombardi Trophy after the Ravens held off the 49ers, 34-31, to win Super Bowl XLVII in February 2013 at the Mercedes-Benz Superdome in New Orleans. "Daddy gets to come home now," Lewis said. "It is the most ultimate feeling ever. This is the way you do it. No other way to go out and end a career. This is how you do it." *Lloyd Fox | Baltimore Sun Photo*

'My last ride': Lewis says he's retiring after the playoffs

BY CHILDS WALKER AND JEFF ZREBIEC · JANUARY 3, 2013 · THE BALTIMORE SUN

Ray Lewis, the face of the Ravens since he played in the franchise's first game at Memorial Stadium and perhaps the greatest linebacker in NFL history, will make this year's playoff run his last.

Lewis, who expects to return from a torn triceps for Sunday's AFC wild-card game against the Indianapolis Colts, announced the impending end of his 17-year career to a roomful of stunned teammates Wednesday morning at the Ravens' practice facility in Owings Mills.

"I told my team that this would be my last ride," Lewis said, startling listeners at a news conference after he had spent a few minutes answering routine questions about his injury. "And I told them I was just at so much peace in where I am with my decision, because of everything I've done in this league. I've done it. I've done it, man. There's no accolade that I don't have individually."

Lewis' biography is one of extremes. A child of a broken home, he became a football prodigy, seemingly destined for the Hall of Fame from early in his career. Then, just as he neared his pinnacle, he faced murder charges that threatened his future. Lewis pleaded guilty to a lesser charge and he became one of the NFL's most divisive players – derided in opposing cities, deeply respected by his peers, adopted wholeheartedly by Baltimore, the city where he played his whole career and devoted his charitable efforts.

A fiery leader, he riled up teammates and home fans like no one else with his signature entry dance at M&T Bank Stadium. He ended up, finally, as an elder statesman, a sort of wise uncle to the generations who followed him into the nation's most popular sport.

A subdued Lewis said he came to his decision while spending time with his sons as he rehabilitated his injury in Florida. A man of outspoken faith, he talked of growing up without a father and not wanting his children to be without him any longer. He had to choose between them and holding on to the game.

"My children have made the ultimate sacrifice for their father – the ultimate sacrifice for 17 years," he said. "I've done what I wanted to do in this business, and now it is my turn. It's my turn to give them back something."

Though talk of Lewis' potential retirement had become common at the end of each season, the reality hit his teammates hard.

Some were still stunned when they recounted the meeting where Lewis informed them of his decision. For them, as for many fans, it's hard to imagine the Ravens without No. 52 dancing out of the tunnel, without the man underneath the jersey as a wise shoulder to lean on in the locker room.

"Today, I definitely didn't prepare for it," said running back Ray Rice, holding back tears. "Mentally, he has raised me over the last couple of years. My locker is right next to his, and I just can't picture Baltimore without him. He has kids, but I was one of his kids."

Lewis' retirement, along with the possible departure of safety Ed Reed, could signal a radical changing of the guard for a franchise built on stifling defense. That change had already begun this season, as the triceps injury held Lewis out of 10 games and the Ravens fell to 17th in the league in yards allowed.

He wanted to make his intentions clear before Sunday's game, Lewis said, so all Baltimore would feel the moment when he bursts from the tunnel

▶Lewis listens to a question at the news conference at which he announced that he'll retire after the Ravens' playoff run. "I told my team that this would be my last ride," he said. "And I told them I was just at so much peace in where I am with my decision." *Lloyd Fox | Baltimore Sun Photo*

in his traditional dance, hips swiveling and chest thrust out at the world.

"I think my fans, my city, they deserve it," he said. "I think we will all get to enjoy what Sunday will feel like, knowing that this will be the last time 52 plays in a uniform in Ravens stadium."

Accolades poured in from around the league and the wider sporting world as news spread that one of the faces of an NFL generation would walk away.

"A guy you could count on, a guy you could lean on, a guy that gave everything, every free moment that he had to help others, to help the city," said Colts coach Chuck Pagano, who will oppose Lewis on Sunday after working as Ravens defensive coordinator last season. "He's there to serve, and he's done it in numerous ways, and his legacy will live on forever – not only in that city but in the NFL annals. He will go to the Hall of Fame, and he'll go down as one of the greatest, if not the greatest, to play the position."

Lewis' ride to greatness was hardly gentle. In 2000, just as he entered his playing prime, he was charged with first-degree murder in connection with the stabbing deaths of two men outside an Atlanta club. After two weeks of a summer trial, he pleaded guilty to a misdemeanor obstruction-of-justice charge after agreeing to testify against two former co-defendants. The incident would forever provide fodder for opposing fans, who booed Lewis lustily in enemy stadiums. But he turned his lowest moment into the stage for his greatest, leading the Ravens to victory in Super Bowl XXXV after one of the finest seasons ever by a defensive player.

With his unmatched style of prowling from sideline to sideline and his fiery pregame speeches, delivered in a sonorous preacher's voice, Lewis joined the pantheon of Baltimore sports heroes. What Johnny Unitas had been to generations of Colts fans, Lewis became to the city's new wave of football lovers, now clad in purple.

Lewis focused his charitable efforts heavily on Baltimore, along with his home state of Florida, establishing the Ray Lewis Family Foundation to distribute money to disadvantaged youths, providing free school supplies to thousands of city students and dispensing Thanksgiving meals, Christmas gifts and winter garments

to hundreds more families. In 2010, the city rechristened a stretch of North Avenue "Ray Lewis Way."

And then he played on and on, longer than any linebacker currently in the Pro Football Hall of Fame, where Lewis is sure to be enshrined after a five-year wait. In recent years, he played with and against players who had grown up using him as a character in video games.

"'He definitely inspired me," said Minnesota Vikings running back Adrian Peterson. "Just the passion and how he is dedicated to his craft to be the best. You don't see too many guys who play like that. That's definitely what makes him the best linebacker to ever play the game."

From the beginning

After a decorated career at the University of Miami, Lewis, a native of Lakeland, Fla., was the second player ever selected by the Ravens, 26th overall in the 1996 NFL draft. By picking Lewis and offensive tackle Jonathan Ogden in the first round, now-general manager Ozzie Newsome laid the foundation for one of the league's most talent-rich organizations.

"Ray Lewis will not only be remembered as one of the greatest to play his position, he will also be thought of as one of the greatest players in NFL history," said Newsome, himself a Hall of Fame player. "And he is one of the greatest without a doubt. He had the one quality all of the best have: He made all the players, coaches and people around him better."

Lewis started from his first game, in which he recorded an interception against the Oakland Raiders, and by his third season, he was already regarded as one of the top defensive players in the league. He would go on to be named the NFL's Defensive Player of the Year twice and to make 13 Pro Bowls.

The past two seasons have been difficult for Lewis, who was too often relegated to a cheerleading and mentoring role on the sidelines. He missed four games with a toe injury last season and even before he went down, he struggled to keep up with running backs or discard blocks as he had in the past.

As soon as he tore his triceps Oct. 14 against the Dallas Cowboys, national football commentators began contemplating the end of Lewis' career. The injury is usually season-ending. And many wondered whether the

Fans hold up Lewis' jersey number during the AFC wild-card game in January 2013. "I think we will all get to enjoy what Sunday will feel like, knowing that this will be the last time 52 plays in a uniform in Ravens stadium," he said in announcing his retirement plans. *Dylan Slagle | Baltimore Sun Photo*

37-year-old Lewis would want to gear up for another run.

This thinking seemed naive to those who have studied Lewis closely during his time in Baltimore. This is a man who vowed to return for a 17th season mere moments after the Ravens suffered an agonizing loss in last year's AFC championship game.

With that defeat still fresh, he began working out – biking and swimming – as many as seven times a day. He rebuilt his diet around purified juice concoctions and showed up for training camp looking as trim and youthful as he had in a decade. Lewis scoffed at the notion that preparing for a season had gotten harder with age.

Would this man, for whom the will to be great is as old hat as breathing, let an injury dictate his ending? Not likely.

Lewis said he was up on his bicycle 10 days after the triceps surgery with absolute determination to return for a last playoff run, an intention he conveyed with a phone call to Newsome. "I told Ozzie, 'We need to talk, because I'm not going out like this,' " Lewis recalled.

He has been back at practice for almost a month now, and his locker-room demeanor has offered little hint that retirement might be looming. From his familiar corner perch next to Rice, Lewis woofed and hurled good-natured insults across the room, the muscles of his torso a marvel for a guy approaching middle age.

▲Lewis goes through his pregame ritual dance before a preseason game against the Redskins in August 2011 at M&T Bank Stadium, sliding his feet, clapping, gyrating, swiveling his hips and thrusting out his chest as if an NFL championship were on the line. *Gene Sweeney, Jr. | Baltimore Sun Photo*

But make no mistake: Lewis is an old man in professional football years. As he winds toward the end, consider the sweep of his career.

The test of time

Start by looking at the guys he played with when the Ravens debuted in Baltimore in 1996. Most have been out of the league for a decade or more. Ogden is up for the Hall of Fame this year. Even ageless kicker Matt Stover hasn't put his foot to a ball since 2009.

Check out some of Lewis' linebacking partners over the years. Jamie Sharper and Peter Boulware, both of whom joined him in his second year, have

been retired since 2005. Adalius Thomas, who briefly surpassed Lewis in the eyes of some, hasn't played since 2009.

It feels only natural to associate Lewis and Reed, the veteran pillars of the Ravens' defense. But Lewis had played six seasons and established himself as the best defender in the game before Reed ever donned an NFL jersey.

"He's amazing," Boulware said. "A lot of guys who play a long time, you see their productivity slip, but he really hasn't dropped off that much. He's one of the greatest linebackers to ever play the game."

Teammates talked of soaking up his wisdom in the last few weeks he's around. "You take it for granted having someone like him on the team," said

Pro Bowl defensive tackle Haloti Ngata, a teammate since 2006. "When he told us, I started thinking about things I could probably ask him or try to pick his brain about, how to be great not only on the field but off the field."

Such longevity rarely leads to happy endings in sports. But Lewis has largely avoided the ignominy of the faded legend – Unitas wearing No. 19 for the San Diego Chargers, Muhammad Ali getting pounded against the ropes by Larry Holmes, Michael Jordan struggling to dunk in a Washington Wizards jersey.

Lewis always said he would know when it was time to go.

On Wednesday, he offered few hints of what would come next, though he said, "It's a new chapter that I've already pre-planned out."

He'll be there to watch his son, Ray Lewis III, play at Miami next season. He has been a national pitchman for products such as Under Armour apparel, Old Spice deodorant and EA Sports video games and has long been talked about as a possible television analyst. He also delivers inspirational speeches to everyone from church congregations to small-college athletic teams.

Lewis appeared utterly calm about his decision as he spoke of God calling him to the next phase of his life.

"The emotions are very controlled, because I never redo one day," he said. "Every moment I've ever had in this building, what this organization has done for me, what this city has done for me, what my fans have done for me, what the mutual respect for different players have done for me around this league, I can never take any of that back. That's the ultimate when you leave this game. You leave it with one heck of a legacy." ∎

No. 52 the greatest ever to play middle linebacker

BY MIKE PRESTON · JANUARY 3, 2013 · THE BALTIMORE SUN

There is really only one more appropriate ending for Ray Lewis, and that won't come for five more years, when he takes his place in the Pro Football Hall of Fame as the greatest middle linebacker ever.

Lewis, 37, announced yesterday that he will retire at the end of the Ravens' season, and even though it was a sad day for Baltimore sports fans, it was a great one, too.

Unlike Johnny Unitas, the city's other legendary football player, Lewis gets to end his career in a Baltimore uniform. No other hometown fan base will be revved up by his introductory dance, which will be on display one more time when the Ravens host the Indianapolis Colts in an AFC wild-card game at M&T Bank Stadium.

Often in sports we use the word "great," but that should be reserved for players who transcend the game and reinvent their position.

That was Ray Lewis, No. 52.

There have been other great ones, such as the Chicago Bears' Dick Butkus and Mike Singletary, but none was the complete package like Lewis.

"I think Butkus was the best at stopping the run, but Ray Lewis could stop the run or get back in to play pass defense," said former Baltimore Colts running back Tom Matte, who played against most of the top middle linebackers. "He had such speed and agility. I'm prejudiced, of course, but there was none better.

"I'm happy to see him retiring as a Raven. He is the last of a dying breed, a player who never wanted to play anywhere else."

Lewis was exceptional because he was the first middle linebacker who could run sideline to sideline and still cover a tight end or running back one-on-one down the field. He studied and prepared for every game as if it were his last, and he made others around him great.

It didn't seem as though Lewis would make this incredible Hall of Fame journey when he arrived in Baltimore 17 years ago. On his first day here, he sat in the hall at the team's old training facility in Owings Mills wearing dark sunglasses, a blue pinstriped suit and gold chains around his neck. He looked like he weighed about 220 pounds.

"That is going to be your middle linebacker?" I asked Ravens general manager Ozzie Newsome. "Damn, he is skinny."

"Yes," Newsome replied. "Wait till you see the finished product."

Since then, he has been selected to 13 Pro Bowls, won a Super Bowl, been named Super Bowl Most Valuable Player and received two NFL Defensive

▶A fan decked out in Ravens colors holds up a sign showing his appreciation for Lewis during the first half of the middle linebacker's final game at M&T Bank Stadium, a 24-9 AFC wild-card win over the Colts in January 2013. *Dylan Slagle | Baltimore Sun Photo*

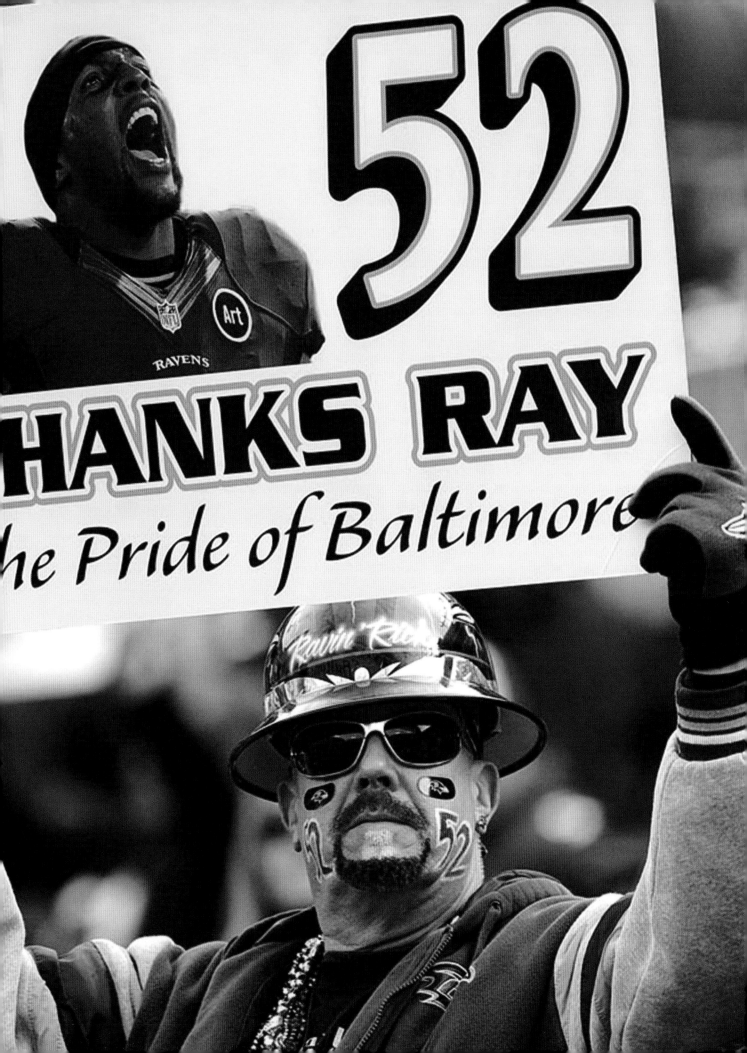

Player of the Year Awards. Lewis is just the sixth player in NFL history to win Player of the Year more than once, and the only middle linebacker other than Singletary.

And here's something else that separates Lewis from the others: He played 17 years. Few of the great ones come close to his longevity.

There are other intangibles that made Lewis great. When Lewis was in his prime, Ravens coaches Ted Marchibroda and Brian Billick had to slow him in practice because he always played at game speed.

Lewis challenged his teammates to be great and often delivered fiery versions of a speech titled "Where Would You Rather Be?" before big games.

"He never disappointed," said Cincinnati Bengals coach Marvin Lewis, Lewis' first defensive coordinator in Baltimore. "He always said he wanted to learn the game as a coach, and he was motivated to be the best. He made everybody else better, and he took the leadership role on his shoulders even as a young player."

Through 17 years, Lewis left a trail of battered bodies. In 2008, Lewis tackled Pittsburgh Steelers running back Rashard Mendenhall so hard that he broke Mendenhall's collarbone. Against Cincinnati in 2000, Lewis was so destructive on the field that running back Corey Dillon declined to go back into the game late in the fourth quarter.

The turning point in Lewis' career came Sept. 29, 1997, when San Diego Chargers running back Eric Metcalf caught a pass in the left flat and darted over the middle. Lewis changed direction and ran down Metcalf after a 62-yard gain.

Metcalf had been timed in the 40-yard dash in 4.3 seconds, but Lewis caught him and pulled him down with one hand. Middle linebackers weren't supposed to run that fast.

That's when you knew the Ravens had something special in No. 52.

Through the years, I've had a good relationship with Lewis. There have been some rocky times in the past couple of seasons because I saw a player starting to lose some attributes that had made him great.

But in every practice I've attended since the team moved here for the 1996 season, and there have been many, I always took some time to watch Lewis and, until he retired, Hall of Fame offensive tackle Jonathan Ogden.

That was my privilege, my honor, to watch greatness at work.

I often wondered how this on-field marriage between Lewis and the Ravens would end. I didn't want to see him go out like Unitas, gimpy-legged and wearing a Chargers uniform.

I'm glad to see Lewis come back from injury. I'm glad he'll come out of the tunnel one more time to dance because it's something we all can savor.

It's fitting for the fans, the city and Ray Lewis, the greatest middle linebacker ever to play the game. ∎

▶Lewis and quarterback Joe Flacco (left) gaze at a flyover before the Ravens' wild-card game against the Colts in January 2013. Lewis announced four days earlier that he would retire at the end of the Ravens' postseason run.
Karl Merton Ferron | Baltimore Sun Photo

TEN
Memorable Moments

BY MATT VENSEL · JANUARY 3, 2013 · THE BALTIMORE SUN

In a legendary professional career spanning 17 seasons, Ravens inside linebacker Ray Lewis has made countless big plays, including momentum-changing takeaways, teeth-rattling hits and game-saving tackles. Here are 10 of our favorite Lewis moments, listed in chronological order:

#1 Heck of a pro debut

Sept. 1, 1996 (Ravens beat Raiders, 19-14): In his first game in the NFL, the first-round draft pick out of Miami made seven tackles and picked off Billy Joe Hobert in the Memorial Stadium end zone.

#2 This kid's got wheels

Sept. 28, 1997 (Chargers beat Ravens, 21-17): San Diego got the win, but the second-year linebacker opened eyes when he chased down wide receiver Eric Metcalf from 15 yards behind.

#3 'Folded up like a baby'

Nov. 12, 2000 (Ravens beat Titans, 24-23): In a big win during their title season, Lewis hit Tennessee running back Eddie George so hard that cornerback Chris McAlister said George had "folded up like a baby."

#4 Pick-six in Tennessee

Jan. 7, 2001 (Ravens beat Titans, 24-10): Lewis sealed a playoff win over Tennessee when he intercepted a pass from Steve McNair that was bobbled by George and returned it 50 yards for a score.

#5 Super performance

Jan. 28, 2001 (Ravens beat Giants, 34-7): Lewis was named the Most Valuable Player of Super Bowl XXXV after he made 11 tackles and tipped a pass from Kerry Collins that was intercepted by Jamie Sharper.

#6 Springing McAlister

Sept. 30, 2002 (Ravens beat Broncos, 34-23): While McAlister returned a missed field-goal attempt 108 yards for a touchdown, Lewis landed a crushing block on Keith Burns.

#7 Welcome, Rookie

Sept. 29, 2008 (Steelers beat Ravens, 23-20): Lewis ended the rookie season of Pittsburgh running back Rashard Mendenhall after just three games, fracturing his shoulder with a crushing hit.

#8 Stuffing Sproles

Sept. 20, 2009 (Ravens beat Chargers, 31-26): Lewis stopped a late San Diego rally on fourth-and-2 by shooting through their offensive line to tackle running back Darren Sproles for a 5-yard loss.

#9 Down goes Brady

Jan. 10, 2010 (Ravens beat Patriots, 33-14): Early in the playoff pounding of New England, Lewis blitzed quarterback Tom Brady up the gut and jumped on his back for a tone-setting sack.

#10 Decleating Dustin

Sept. 13, 2010 (Ravens beat Jets, 10-9): Lewis helped finish off a season-opening win by drilling Dustin Keller with a hard, clean hit as the New York tight end tried to catch a pass over the middle. ∎

▶Gary McHugh Jr. of Pasadena lifts a giant Lewis head over the crowd gathered on the field at M&T Bank Stadium in February 2013 to celebrate the Ravens' second Super Bowl victory. Lewis – the man, not the cutout – performed his trademark "Squirrel" dance during the ceremony. *Kim Hairston | Baltimore Sun Photo*

Lewis' 13 tackles in final home game send Ravens to second round of playoffs

BY JEFF ZREBIEC · JANUARY 7, 2013 · THE BALTIMORE SUN

Ray Lewis ran onto the field one more time, and the man who has written the Ravens' defensive record book had another career first left in him. As quarterback Joe Flacco prepared to kneel, Lewis jogged about 10 yards behind him and took his place in the victory formation.

Once Flacco took the final snap and handed the ball to referee Mike Carey, Lewis did his trademark dance. This was indeed Lewis' day. He had earned that much in the final home game of his 17 seasons, all with one franchise.

But when it was over, the Ravens rushed onto the field to celebrate the continuation of not just Lewis' Hall of Fame-worthy career, but their season. A 24-9 victory over the Indianapolis Colts in front of an announced 71,379 at M&T Bank Stadium sends the Ravens into the second round of the playoffs, where they will meet a Denver Broncos team that embarrassed them by 17 points in Baltimore three weeks ago.

The Ravens and Broncos will play at Sports Authority Field at 4:30 p.m. Saturday, and a win would get the Ravens into the AFC championship game for a second straight season. As it is, the Ravens have now won a playoff game in five straight seasons. John Harbaugh is the first coach since the 1970 AFL-NFL merger to earn a postseason victory in his first five seasons at the helm.

"I think we're all appreciative, grateful for the opportunity to be here and to witness this historic moment in sports," said Harbaugh, who is now 6-4 in the postseason, including 4-0 in wild-card games. "It wasn't just about one guy. Nobody understands it more than the one guy we're talking about. It was about a team. It was about a city, a fan base, about a great sport, about a great career. I'm just humbled to be part of it."

Lewis, who announced Wednesday that this playoff run would be his "last ride," took a victory lap around M&T Bank Stadium reminiscent of former Oriole Cal Ripken Jr.'s celebration at Camden Yards after he broke Lou Gehrig's streak for consecutive games played. In his first game since he tore his right triceps Oct. 14, Lewis was credited with a game-high 13 tackles.

"It probably won't sink in," Lewis said when asked about never getting to play at M&T Bank Stadium again. "You know what, the reason is because the next thing on my mind is, as a team, we are poised to go do something. As men, we made a commitment to each other, and that is to head next week to Denver to get a win."

By the time pregame introductions began, there wasn't an open seat to be

▸Lewis drops an easy interception in the second quarter on a pass thrown by Colts rookie quarterback Andrew Luck. "I'll never live that one down," the middle linebacker said with a laugh. "I'm going to blame that one on the [arm] brace." *Lloyd Fox | Baltimore Sun Photo*

found. After Ed Reed's name was announced – the safety also might have played his last home game as a Raven – Lewis came out and did his signature "Squirrel" dance as teammates rushed toward him. Flacco joked that he tried to persuade his wife, Dana, to bring in a video camera to capture the moment. Harbaugh also inched forward to get a good view.

Although Lewis showed some signs of rust, the 37-year-old had a solid game overall.

In the second quarter, though, Lewis bobbled a pass by Andrew Luck, the Colts rookie quarterback, that defensive tackle Haloti Ngata deflected. The drop prompted groans from the stands.

"I'll never live that one down," Lewis said with a laugh. "I'm going to put that one on the brace because I tried to put my arm up, but the brace wouldn't come up."

Lewis indicated that he didn't suffer any setbacks with the arm injury and didn't demonstrate any glaring problems.

Said cornerback Cary Williams: "He was himself. He was the same guy you've seen for the last 17 years. He was a professional."

Mostly Lewis was Lewis.

"I thought he played exceptionally well," Harbaugh said. "It's always funny to hear people say, 'Well, he's not the same that [he] was 10 years ago.' Well, who is? None of us, but he's found different ways to play the game and play it so well. He's still a great football player."

During the final minutes of the game, the Ravens saluted Lewis with a montage of his top career moments.

"It was a bunch of tears," said Pro Bowl running back Ray Rice, who's been mentored by Lewis. "It was sort of like, 'Save the Last Dance.' "

About an hour after the game and his victory lap, Lewis said he would allow his teammates to enjoy the victory for no more than 12 hours. Lewis had already turned in his iPad so it could be loaded with game film of Peyton Manning and the Broncos. Ravens fans might never forget Lewis' final home game, but the 37-year-old linebacker had already moved on.

"At the end of the day, it's not about me and Peyton. It's about their team against our team," Lewis said. "I just like our team. I love our team right now, and I'm really looking forward to going out there and playing them next week." ∎

▶Lewis takes a Cal Ripken Jr.-like lap around M&T Bank Stadium after playing his final game there and helping the Ravens earn a berth in the AFC divisional round. *Dylan Slagle | Baltimore Sun Photo*

Lewis, Ravens survive double-overtime thriller in Denver to reach AFC title game

BY JEFF ZREBIEC · JANUARY 13, 2013 · THE BALTIMORE SUN

When the best game that almost every Ravens player had ever been a part of was finally over, Joe Flacco thrust up his hands, Justin Tucker pumped his fist and Ray Lewis dropped to his knees, reduced to tears.

Tucker's 47-yard field goal 1:42 into the second quarter of overtime ended a thrilling and exhausting divisional round playoff game and sent the Ravens into the AFC championship game for the second straight year. The 38-35 victory over the host Denver Broncos earns the Ravens a date with the winner of today's game between the New England Patriots and the Houston Texans.

"When all the emotions calm down, it will probably be one of the greatest victories in Ravens history," said Lewis, whose retirement tour will extend at least one more week.

It also might be one of their most improbable victories. The Ravens allowed two return touchdowns to Trindon Holliday, who became the first player in NFL history to accomplish that feat in the postseason, and they trailed by a touchdown with the ball at their own 30 and under a minute to go in regulation.

Flacco, who played one of his best games as a professional quarterback, spotted Jacoby Jones down the right sideline behind the Broncos defense and unleashed a ball that seemingly hung in the air forever. Having beaten Tony Carter and Rahim Moore, Jones caught it and sprinted into the end zone for a 70-yard touchdown with 31 seconds to play.

"I've never seen anything like that," said Ravens wide receiver Torrey Smith who had two touchdown catches and outplayed Broncos star cornerback Champ Bailey. "You play some games on 'Madden' and you can't even do that."

The two teams traded punts to open overtime, but on the Broncos' second possession Peyton Manning threw across his body and was intercepted by cornerback Corey Graham, giving the Ravens the ball at the Denver 45. An 11-yard run by Ray Rice put Tucker into position to convert the game-winner.

Saturday's was the longest game in Lewis' 17-year career, and with 17 tackles – one for each year of his Hall of Fame career, he was savoring every moment.

"I've never been a part of a game so crazy in my life," Lewis said.

Naturally, he took his time dressing before he came out, and apologized for keeping the media waiting.

He was keeping someone else waiting, too.

Manning was waiting around to congratulate Lewis, and the victor was especially gracious.

"There's so much respect I have for Peyton," Lewis said. He hadn't beaten him since early in the previous decade.

"Nine straight losses," Lewis reflected. "I didn't think about it. I just heard about it. I heard about it so many times."

When he thought about the game, Lewis grew reflective.

"When all the emotions calm down, it will probably be one of the greatest victories in Ravens history, and that's probably because of how things were stacked up against us," he said.

His obligations finally done, Lewis got ready for a happy flight.

"The plane ride is going to be so awesome," Lewis said. ∎

Rich Dubroff of the Carroll County Times contributed to this article.

▶Lewis (left) and Pernell McPhee celebrate after McPhee forced Broncos quarterback Peyton Manning to fumble in the third quarter of the Ravens' 38-35, double-overtime road win in the AFC divisional round in January 2013; Paul Kruger, a linebacker like Lewis and McPhee, recovered for Baltimore. *Lloyd Fox | Baltimore Sun Photo*

Ray-venge: Lewis makes 14 tackles in win over Patriots for AFC title

BY AARON WILSON · JANUARY 21, 2013 · THE BALTIMORE SUN

Ray Lewis knelt on the field and put his head on the ground, practically attaching himself to the turf in complete jubilation.

Surrounded by his adoring teammates, the retiring middle linebacker was overcome with emotion after the Ravens' 28-13 victory over the New England Patriots on Sunday night in the AFC championship game at Gillette Stadium in Foxborough, Mass.

For Lewis, it was a triumph of will after telling his teammates that he would be back on the field alongside them after tearing his right triceps in October against the Dallas Cowboys.

Not only did Lewis return from a major injury after undergoing surgery and a grueling rehabilitation, but the two-time NFL Defensive Player of the Year is now headed to the Super Bowl in New Orleans to square off with the San Francisco 49ers.

"There's something special in our locker room," Lewis said. "There's a certain type of love we have for each other. For me to come out and say this was my last ride and for me to be heading back to the Super Bowl for the possibility of a second ring, how else do you cap off a career?

"How else do you honor your fans and give them everything you cheer for? Baltimore is one of the most loyal places I've been around since 1996. The greatest reward you can give them is another chance at a Super Bowl. The last ride, I can only say I'm along for the ride."

Weeks after announcing that this would be the final season of his stellar NFL career after 17 seasons, the former Super Bowl Most Valuable Player is leaving the game in dramatic fashion.

Now, Lewis' unfinished business is trying to win his second Super Bowl ring more than a decade after the Ravens' win over the New York Giants in Super Bowl XXXV.

"It's awesome that we can give our general an opportunity to go to the Super Bowl in his final year," cornerback Cary Williams said. "Ray has been a tremendous leader for this organization, for this community. It's an honor to even be a teammate of his. He's going to go down as the greatest of all time. What a great way to send him out with a Super Bowl trip."

Whether it was Ravens majority owner Steve Bisciotti, coach John Harbaugh or other Baltimore sports figures like Olympic swimming champion Michael Phelps or Orioles center fielder Adam Jones, tribute was paid to Lewis after defeating a Patriots team headlined by quarterback Tom Brady.

"The coolest thing is watching the amount of emotion and leadership Ray Lewis has," Phelps said. "I can't say enough about the passion that Ray Lewis has. It's one of the most incredible things I've seen in my entire life. When Big Ray and Little Ray [running back Ray Rice] were hugging on the field, I broke down in tears. The amount of love and respect I have for him, I'm literally on cloud nine."

Lewis recorded a game-high 14 tackles, giving him 44 in three playoff games since returning from an injury that was initially expected to end his season.

The 37-year-old didn't make many high-impact plays, but he played his traditional role by providing leadership and hard-nosed

▶Defensive tackle Haloti Ngata (left) and Lewis stop Patriots running back Shane Vereen for no gain in the first quarter of the Ravens' 28-13 win in the AFC championship game in January 2013 in Foxborough, Mass. Lewis had 14 tackles, giving him 44 in the team's first three postseason games. *Gene Sweeney Jr. | Baltimore Sun Photo*

tackling against the run and quarterbacking his defense into the right strategic moves.

One year ago on this same field where so many other worthy football teams have come up short, the Ravens lost the AFC championship.

They were defeated, 23-20, as kicker Billy Cundiff flubbed a chip-shot field-goal attempt and wide receiver Lee Evans mishandled a potential game-winning touchdown pass that was ripped out of his hands by Sterling Moore.

Lewis recalled the feeling and his words to his teammates from a year ago compared with how they're feeling now.

"After that game, my speech, that moment, that conversation I had with my team, I remember telling them, 'God doesn't make mistakes. He's never made one mistake,' " Lewis recalled. "Last year, we ran our course. We came back and faced with adversity, there was no way God was going to bring us back here twice to feel the same feeling. He had a real plan for us the whole year. I congratulate my team. We stuck to the course. It was always 'Next man up.' We're back and we're on our way to the Super Bowl." ▪

▶(From left) Lewis, outside linebacker Terrell Suggs, running back Ray Rice and fullback Vonta Leach celebrate with the Lamar Hunt Trophy after winning the AFC championship. "I congratulate my team," Lewis said. "We stuck to the course. It was always 'Next man up.' We're back and we're on our way to the Super Bowl." *Kenneth K. Lam | Baltimore Sun Photo*

Again the center of attention, Lewis faced questions from the national media before Super Bowl XLVII in New Orleans about his alleged use of a banned hormone to aid his recovery from a torn triceps. *Gene Sweeney, Jr. | Baltimore Sun Photo*

Lewis rides off into sunset with Super Bowl victory over 49ers

BY CHILDS WALKER · FEBRUARY 4, 2013 · THE BALTIMORE SUN

Ray Lewis' Ravens held on for dear life, a seemingly certain Super Bowl victory only a few yards from slipping away.

In the end, however, Lewis got the finale he wanted to his decorated 17-year career, a world championship secured by one last defensive stand against the younger, faster San Francisco 49ers.

When it was finally over, Lewis bellowed at the sky, his arms wide open as confetti rained around him. The face of the Ravens was a Super Bowl champion for the second time and a retiree for the first.

"Baltimore!" he shouted, clutching the Lombardi Trophy.

"It's simple," Lewis said when CBS announcer Jim Nantz asked him what he made of the victory. "When God is for you, who can be against you?"

He had announced that this was his "last ride" just before the playoffs, when few gave the Ravens a chance to go all the way. In the days that followed, some teammates would say the emotional announcement was the turning point in their season.

Lewis' last game was also perhaps his strangest. The Ravens jumped to a 28-6 lead only to sacrifice almost all of it after a 33-minute power outage struck the Mercedes-Benz Superdome in New Orleans early in the third quarter. After the lights returned, Lewis' defense could hardly slow the 49ers.

Before all the insanity, Lewis gave Ravens fans some vintage moments.

With black triangles painted under his eyes, he gathered his teammates around him one last time, thrusting his face into theirs as he woofed pregame inspiration. The Ravens' faithful chanted "Seven Nation Army" in the background.

Lewis panted with emotion as Alicia Keys sang the national anthem. Once the game began, he was his usual lively self, strutting and flapping his arms to the crowd every time he got in on a hit.

But there were reminders that this wasn't the Lewis of 2000. When 49ers quarterback Colin Kaepernick took off running, the 37-year-old Lewis wasn't quick enough to close on him. And he could not cover tight end Vernon Davis, who caught six passes on eight targets for 104 yards.

Quarterback Joe Flacco, whom Lewis had anointed "the general" earlier in the playoffs, was the clear star for Baltimore.

Ultimately the Ravens' defense made the defining stand late in the game, Lewis barking directions when it mattered most.

"The final series of Ray Lewis' career was a goal-line stand to win the Lombardi Trophy," Ravens coach John Harbaugh said. "Ray said it on the podium: How could it be any other way than that?"

The last week of Lewis' career was just as complicated as the previous 17 years. Amid all the plaudits for his greatness came allegations in a Sports Illustrated article that he had obtained performance-enhancing drugs to aid his recovery from a torn triceps. Lewis adamantly denied using deer antler spray – laced with a banned hormone according to its maker.

But the story gave critics new ammunition to question Lewis' self-image as a morally upright warrior.

Baltimore fans have never paid Lewis' detractors much mind. For them he'll always be the face of a pro football renaissance that began in 1996, 12 years after the Colts had broken their hearts by fleeing town.

The stats and accolades say plenty about Lewis: 17 seasons, more than any linebacker currently in the Pro Football Hall of Fame, 13 Pro Bowl

▶Lewis tackles 49ers wide receiver Michael Crabtree late in the fourth quarter of the Super Bowl in February 2013. Lewis finished with seven tackles, his lowest total during the postseason run, then revealed three years later that he had retorn his triceps the night before the game. *Lloyd Fox | Baltimore Sun Photo*

Lewis surveys the 49ers offense during the first half. The veteran linebacker struggled to keep up with mobile quarterback Colin Kaepernick (7), but he helped anchor a goal-line stand at the end of the game that made the Ravens champions again. *Dylan Slagle | Baltimore Sun Photo*

selections, Super Bowl MVP, NFL All-Decade.

But it's the images that will really abide.

Just as Baltimoreans remember Johnny Unitas, coolly cocking the ball during a fourth-quarter comeback, they will forever dream of the young No. 52, dashing from sideline to sideline to corral every ballcarrier in sight. They'll picture the hips shimmying and the chest thrusting as Lewis emerged from the tunnel at M&T Bank Stadium to the beats of Nelly's "Hot in Herre." They'll recall the fire in his eyes and the music in his voice as he barked at teammates, "Any dogs in the house?"

It's a complicated legacy to be sure. Around the country, many have never gotten past the murder charges Lewis faced in connection with the fatal stabbing of two men outside an Atlanta club the night of the 2000 Super Bowl. He pleaded guilty to a misdemeanor obstruction-of-justice charge and agreed to testify against his co-defendants, later reaching financial settlements with the families of both victims to avoid civil trials.

Lewis stood in the eye of a media storm as he led the Ravens to the Super Bowl in January 2001, a year after the Atlanta incident. He wasn't asked about it nearly as much this year, though when he was, he said he lives with it every day.

Atlanta aside, other fans see Lewis as a phony because of his outspoken Christianity and showy leadership.

His hold on a football nation is undeniable, however. No other player's jersey was close to as prevalent on the streets of New Orleans in the past week. And stars from around the NFL have paid verbal homage to Lewis, not only as an on-field force but as a personal counselor on the travails of public life.

For a few moments on Sunday night, all the complexity washed away and Lewis was just a man who had given his life to football, celebrating the perfect ending.

"Daddy gets to come home now," Lewis said. "It is the most ultimate feeling ever. This is the way you do it. No other way to go out and end a career. This is how you do it." ∎

▶Lewis, wearing a commemorative Super Bowl champion cap, kisses Ravens owner Steve Bisciotti on the forehead during the on-field celebration. "He'll always be a Raven and he'll always be around for us," Bisciotti said a month later of the retired Lewis. *Lloyd Fox | Baltimore Sun Photo*

Lewis runs onto the field before the Ravens routed the Texans, 30-9, in September 2013. Lewis was inducted into the team's Ring of Honor at M&T Bank Stadium during a halftime presentation. "The love that's out there in that stadium and the love that this city has for me and the respect the players have for me is overwhelming," Lewis said after the ceremony. *Christopher T. Assaf | Baltimore Sun Photo*

LEGACY AND A CALL TO THE HALL

Ring of Honor ceremony is 'humbling' homecoming for Lewis

BY PETER SCHMUCK · SEPTEMBER 23, 2013 · THE BALTIMORE SUN

For the fans who packed M&T Bank Stadium on Sunday and stayed in their seats at halftime to see Ray Lewis inducted into the Ravens Ring of Honor, it would be hard to imagine a more appropriate way to honor the greatest Raven of them all.

Sure, Lewis got an amazing reception from the announced sellout crowd of 71,168 when he walked onto the field before the game and again during the halftime ceremony that featured an impressive VIP list of Pro Football Hall of Famers and previous Ring of Honor inductees. Sure, he regaled the crowd with an inspirational acceptance speech. That was all great.

What made it unique, however, was the fact that his replacement at middle linebacker, newcomer Daryl Smith, had just turned the game around by intercepting a pass by Houston Texans quarterback Matt Schaub and sprinting into the end zone to give the Ravens their first lead of the game.

"As I walked out of the tunnel, I said, 'I should have run out there and he should have just tossed me the ball,' " Lewis said during a news conference after the ceremony. "Me and Steve [Bisciotti] were walking down and we were like, 'We should have come down earlier to give them some motivation,' but it was so perfect."

The Ravens were represented by owner Bisciotti, club president Dick Cass and general manager Ozzie Newsome. They presented Lewis with an engraved crystal vase and a large oil painting of him in his "Squirrel" dance pose by artist Tim Byrne, the son of Ravens senior vice president of public and community relations Kevin Byrne.

"The love that's out there in that stadium and the love that this city has for me and the respect the players have for me is overwhelming," Lewis said after the ceremony. "It's humbling

Lewis addresses the crowd after being inducted into the Ravens Ring of Honor in September 2013. "This is why you do it," he said of the accolade. "This is why you go through all those hard times."
Christopher T. Assaf | Baltimore Sun Photo

because I only know what the path chose. To see it now ... this is it. This is why you do it. This is why you go through all those hard times."

Lewis clearly reveled in the shower of affection from the stands and projected it right back to the fans he entertained for nearly two decades and - along with his teammates - rewarded with two Super Bowl titles.

"It's good to be back home," he said. "That's one thing I've always said about me being here for 17 years is that I got a chance to lay my head in one place, and if you can have that, that's the foundation of a legacy. So to be back where it all started from is probably one of the greatest gifts I can ever give myself." ∎

In new statue outside stadium, Lewis is larger than life

BY CHILDS WALKER · SEPTEMBER 5, 2014 · THE BALTIMORE SUN

For most of Ray Lewis' 17-year NFL career, his face – eyes burning, mouth bellowing exhortations – was the face of the Ravens.

Johnny Unitas' flinty gaze and stooped shoulders had symbolized pro football for earlier generations of Baltimore fans, and Lewis followed in the great quarterback's footsteps, becoming an icon for the new era of purple-and-black ardor.

The Ravens made that association official Thursday morning, unveiling a bronze statue of the retired linebacker only a few feet from the statue of Unitas that greets visitors outside M&T Bank Stadium.

"I know that here, we feel complete now, honoring arguably the greatest player ever in Johnny ... and he gets to share – we didn't take this lightly – he gets to share the plaza with the greatest linebacker of all time," Ravens owner Steve Bisciotti said before pulling the cover off the sculpture of Lewis.

The muscled bronze captures Lewis in the middle of his famous "Squirrel" dance, which he briefly performed for the hundreds of Ravens fans who attended Thursday's ceremony.

"Honoring me is honoring everybody here," Lewis said near the end of a sprawling, 31-minute speech. "Because everybody here had a hand in me."

The crowd included Lewis' family, former teammates O.J. Brigance, Michael McCrary and Duane Starks, and famous friends such as Under Armour CEO Kevin Plank and swimmer Michael Phelps.

Lewis thanked dozens of people personally, stopping to tell short stories about many of those in attendance. He recalled how his mother, Sunseria, didn't have enough money for equipment when he first signed up for peewee football in 1985. He relied on a $15 loan from a friend to buy his first pair of cleats.

"I made up my mind that day that my mother's tears would become joy," he said Thursday.

Then Lewis, dabbing away his own tears, looked at his mother in the crowd and said, "Mama, we did it."

He wore a Super Bowl ring on each hand at the statue ceremony, where Bisciotti praised him as "the greatest leader in the history of the NFL."

The crowd at the ceremony grew raucous as Lewis led it on an emotional journey through his career. "Whose house?" one man called. "Ray's house!" another replied. Lewis, still thick-shouldered in a dark gray suit, gave the throng a thumbs-up.

"I will forever be a part of this city," he said. ∎

▶Lewis sits in front of a bronze statue of himself that was unveiled in front of the north gates at M&T Bank Stadium in September 2014. "I will forever be a part of this city," he said. *Lloyd Fox | Baltimore Sun Photo*

Lewis marvels at potential fit for 2018 Hall of Fame induction

BY JEFF ZREBIEC · SEPTEMBER 10, 2017 · THE BALTIMORE SUN

Ray Lewis has been approached many times in recent months and congratulated for his pending induction into the Pro Football Hall of Fame. Lewis warns that nothing is official yet and won't be for several months. But as someone who is always looking for a greater meaning, the former Ravens linebacker can't help but marvel at how everything has lined up.

Lewis, who played 17 seasons with the Ravens before retiring after the 2012 campaign, is eligible for the first time to be part of the 2018 Hall of Fame class. He'll learn Feb. 3 whether he's getting in, exactly five years to the day after he played his final NFL game, the Ravens' 34-31 victory over the San Francisco 49ers in Super Bowl XLVII. The next Hall of Fame class will be unveiled on the eve of Super Bowl 52 (LII), the number Lewis made famous in Baltimore.

"I've thought about the symbolism all the way around," Lewis said in a phone interview with The Baltimore Sun. "It's so unique. That's why I sit back and it's like, 'Wait a minute. I could be going in before Super Bowl 52 and on February 3, exactly five years later?' It's one of those moments where you say, 'You know what, son, you may have really did it.' "

Lewis – considered a virtual lock to join the Ravens' first Hall of Famer, Jonathan Ogden, in Canton, Ohio – was selected to the Pro Bowl in 13 of his 17 seasons. He won two NFL Defensive Player of the Year awards and garnered Most Valuable Player honors of Super Bowl XXXV. Lewis is called by many the best defensive player of his generation.

"Based on his performance from the very first game he played in against the Raiders – I think he had 12 tackles and an interception – to the final time he walked off the field as a Super Bowl champion, there's been very few linebackers to do

it better than him," said Phil Savage, the Ravens' director of scouting in 1996 when they made Lewis the 26th overall selection, taking him 22 slots after they took Ogden with their first-ever pick.

The Hall of Fame Selection Committee will cut a preliminary list of nominees to 25 semifinalists in September. That list will be later whittled to 15 finalists. The day before Super Bowl LII, the 46-person selection committee will vote on the inductees.

Lewis' playing record is without blemish. His candidacy might get some significant opposition from the outside because he pleaded guilty in 2000 to obstruction of justice in connection with the stabbing death of two men in Atlanta during Super Bowl XXXIV festivities. However, Hall of Fame bylaws prohibit voters from considering players' off-the-field actions.

"Count me in the camp viewing Ray as one who goes to the front of the line as a lock," said USA Today NFL columnist Jarrett Bell, a Hall of Fame voter. "There's no dispute that he's one of the greatest linebackers in NFL history. I'd anticipate the discussion on Ray will be short because the bylaws for the Hall of Fame stipulate that we consider the on-field impact and not the off-the-field drama.

"While the post-Super Bowl tragedy remains attached to Lewis' story, it should not spill over to the football accomplishments considered for the Hall. Obviously, the voters are human beings with their own interpretations and I can't speak for the entire group. But as was the case in the past with questions about Lawrence Taylor, if voters want to consider the off-the-field situation and defy the bylaws, they would clearly be in the wrong."

At 42 years old, Lewis is keeping himself plenty busy. He's one of the founders of Power52, a solar initiative that also provides training for at-risk

Lewis is flanked by quarterback Joe Flacco (left) and outside linebacker Terrell Suggs as Ravens players receive and display their white-and-yellow gold rings at a ceremony in June 2013 in the team's training facility in Owings Mills. The rings have 243 round-cut diamonds. "It's the ultimate because now it connects us forever," Lewis said.
Karl Merton Ferron | Baltimore Sun Photo

young adults and military veterans. He's involved in the fashion and funding worlds, and also the alcohol and cigar industries. He works as an analyst on Fox Sports 1 and does motivational speaking.

Lewis insists he doesn't miss football. "If I miss it, I've cheated it," he's long said. He doesn't feel like he's been out of the game for five years, though being around six kids frequently reminds him of that.

"Every day wasn't a good day physically. There

were years where I'd have to crawl to the bathroom just to make it. To now be done with the game, to really appreciate the game now, I see these young kids when they're running and I'm like, 'Nope, you all can have it,' " Lewis said. "I train my son, Rayshad. ... We were running up the hill at Oregon Ridge. And we'll be out there and I'd say, 'You've got to go hard. All I got to go is consistent.' I don't have to kill myself no more. I did it."

Lewis concedes that he's spent time thinking

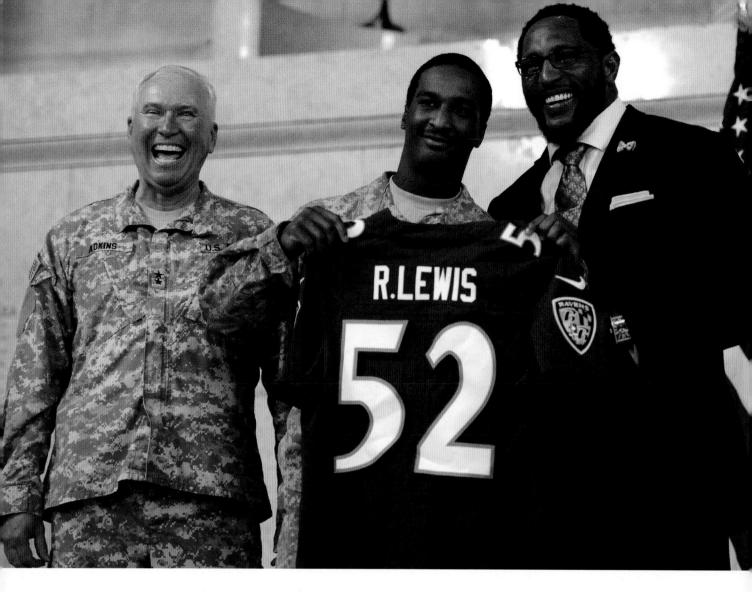

Spc. Darnell Slacum of Baltimore, a member of the 1229th Transportation Company, a unit of the Maryland Army National Guard, is flanked by Maj. Gen. James A. Adkins (left), adjutant general of the Maryland National Guard, and Lewis during a Freedom Salute Ceremony to welcome Slacum's unit home from Afghanistan in September 2014 at the Baltimore War Memorial. *Steve Ruark | Baltimore Sun Photo*

about what it will be like when he's told he's gained entrance into the Hall of Fame.

"When somebody calls you a first-ballot Hall of Famer, that means, in this business, you were the greatest to ever do it," Lewis said. "That's the greatest honor you can ever have. I get it. Getting in is all that matters, but it's the same thing in childhood, when we used to sit out there on the field and somebody would say, 'Who is the captain?' When he picks somebody first, they know that you're that guy. It's that same concept. It's something I never thought could happen when I was younger. It's the greatest honor in this business. It's football heaven."

Lewis said he plans to have his mother, Sunseria Smith, by his side when the 2018 Hall class is unveiled. That's where she's been his whole career, and Lewis says the induction would be the greatest reward he can give her.

Yes, he's also thought briefly about his potential induction speech. There will be plenty of time to formulate that, but Lewis said he's hoping to pay homage to several of his late ex-teammates and opponents, such as Steve McNair, Marlin Barnes, his former roommate at the University of Miami, Derrick Thomas and Sean Taylor. Then, he plans on celebrating the honor with the people he played in front of his entire career.

"The people that I'm going to come back and really celebrate this with are in Baltimore," Lewis said. "That city, the things that we've been through and the things that we keep going through, I want them to really see that you can be the example. Like, it is possible. I'm probably going to have another parade and all of this stuff, but it's going to be amazing." ∎

Fans surround an armored vehicle carrying Lewis near the end of the Super Bowl parade in February 2013. The crowd that gathered to honor the NFL champions was estimated at more than 200,000. *Colby Ware | Baltimore Sun Photo*

Lewis could be inducted into Hall of Fame today

BY JEFF ZREBIEC AND CHILDS WALKER · FEBRUARY 3, 2018 · THE BALTIMORE SUN

His hits landed with an audible thud. His fiery pregame speeches provided motivation for two Super Bowl-winning teams. He was revered in Baltimore and jeered everywhere else.

For 17 seasons, Ray Lewis' NFL career was defined by noise. As he nears entry into the Pro Football Hall of Fame, Lewis finds himself seeking the opposite.

"When the completion of things started to rattle off in my life and I started to take a hard look at what I accomplished, I just want to sit in silence," Lewis, 42, said. "I ride in my car now with silence unless I'm playing jazz music. I don't watch anything on television that confuses where I am right now. I chase so many sunsets."

On Saturday, five years after he played his final game in the Ravens' Super Bowl XLVII victory over the San Francisco 49ers, Lewis is expected to be announced as a member of the Hall of Fame's Class of 2018.

Lewis' candidacy will be reviewed by a selection committee and the conversation about him is expected to be brief. One of the best defensive players of his generation and perhaps the top middle linebacker in NFL history, Lewis is considered a near lock to join fellow 1996 draft pick Jonathan Ogden as the only homegrown Ravens to be enshrined in Canton, Ohio.

"It's the most humbling and nerve-wracking thing you'll ever go through in your life," Lewis said. "If the knock comes on my door, I enter football heaven. I sit with the greats of all greats."

Lewis' career had a humble beginning and a storybook ending. His legacy, though, is complicated.

For many fans outside Baltimore, Lewis' reputation will forever be marred by a 2000 altercation in Atlanta after Super Bowl XXXIV that left two men dead. He was initially charged with murder but eventually pleaded guilty to obstruction of justice. Although he became one of the NFL's most celebrated faces in the aftermath, the specter of Atlanta loomed in national coverage as Lewis announced that he was going to retire and prepared to play his last games in 2013.

Last year, the retired linebacker showed he has not lost his touch for controversy. He interjected himself into the Ravens' debate over signing Colin Kaepernick and subsequently kneeled alongside a dozen Ravens as the U.S. national anthem played before the team's game in London. That action spurred more than 80,000 people to sign a petition calling for owner Steve Bisciotti to remove the statue of Lewis from outside M&T Bank Stadium.

Still, Lewis remains synonymous with the only organization for which he played and helped provide an identity. Lewis' elaborate pregame dance essentially became the official start of a football Sunday in Baltimore.

"Ray is one of the ultimate football players," said Ed Reed, Lewis' longtime Ravens sidekick. "You're talking about a guy who dedicated his time, his effort, his time away from his family, his body for the game of football. Ray knew he was a great football player, and he became a great artist at playing football."

He made the Pro Bowl in 13 of his 17 seasons and was a seven-time first-team All-Pro. Lewis won two NFL Defensive Player of the Year awards and was the MVP of Super Bowl XXXV.

Lewis' impact is revealed by the number of his defensive coordinators and linebacker coaches who got head coaching jobs, his defensive teammates who received big contracts and the next generation of Ravens and other NFL linebackers who patterned their game after him.

"Even to this day, most people identify the Ravens with defense and a lot of that, if not most of it, emanates from what Ray brought to the table. He made a lot of people around him better," said Phil Savage, the Ravens' director of college scouting from 1996 to 2002 and later their director of player

Lewis acknowledges the crowd during a September 2013 ceremony honoring his induction into the Ravens' Ring of Honor at M&T Bank Stadium. Behind him is tackle Jonathan Ogden, who was added in 2008.
Dylan Slagle | Baltimore Sun Photo

personnel. "Ray had a big impact on the league beyond just the playing field. He put people in position to have positions of influence throughout the NFL. He had a quarterback-like impact on the league and that's very difficult to do from the defensive side of the ball."

A diamond in the rough

As a young area scout still finding his footing in 1996, Lionel Vital watched Lewis closely during the 1995 college season. "I've never seen anything like this," he thought. "He was like a one-man gang on a good defense." His initial scouting report, though, was treated with skepticism. Lewis didn't have elite speed and he weighed 220 pounds soaking wet, not an eye-catching combination for an NFL middle linebacker.

But Vital had backing from veteran linebackers coach Maxie Baughan. Weeks before the draft, Baughan traveled to Miami to work Lewis out. The only problem was Lewis was in Tampa. As Miami

Lewis' name is displayed in the Ravens' Ring of Honor at M&T Bank Stadium in September 2013. "It's one of the most humbling feelings that you ever go through," he said of the tribute. *Christopher T. Assaf | Baltimore Sun Photo*

officials tried to reach Lewis, other NFL coaches and scouts grew tired of waiting and left. Not Baughan.

"We kept vigil," Baughan said. "It took a whole day to get that straightened out and I was the one who waited. I'm glad I did."

Baughan asked every linebacker prospect to drop and then pivot as if he were covering a running back up the sideline. Baughan then threw the ball as far as he could to test the linebacker's speed and ball skills. Not once did he get a ball over Lewis' head.

"Only guy in 20 something years that I coached that I couldn't throw it over his head," Baughan said.

The 1996 draft started with a bang for the Ravens. Ogden, the mammoth tackle from UCLA, fell to the fourth pick and vice president of player personnel Ozzie Newsome took him. The Ravens wanted a cog for the middle of their defense with their pick at No. 26. The player they coveted was taken by the Detroit Lions nine spots earlier.

With the Ravens on the clock, Lewis was the best linebacker on their board. But he expected to play somewhere else. Green Bay general manager Ron

Wolf, who was selecting 27th, called to say he'd be selected by the Packers.

"I'm telling everybody in the suite, 'I'm going to be a Green Bay Packer,' " Lewis said. "Next thing you know, the 26th pick is up, and I see my name called. Ozzie Newsome calls and says, 'Ray, this is Ozzie Newsome. Congratulations, I'm drafting you to Baltimore.' "

Lewis and Newsome still joke about Lewis' response. "Baltimore, who?" Lewis asked, a fair question given that the franchise didn't have a name or a logo yet.

Wolf, a Pro Football Hall of Famer and a three-time Super Bowl-winning executive, said he's thought about how his career might have been different if the Packers had gotten Lewis.

"We thought we had him. Lo and behold, those Ravens snuck in there and picked him," Wolf said. "I probably would have been a classified genius had we gotten him, but it wasn't to be. It's fun in this business when your evaluation is correct about a player. Our evaluation of Ray Lewis was right on."

The weekend after the 1996 draft, a group of

Ravens rookies filed off a bus and into the team's Westminster facility and were put through a workout. Most of the rookies struggled through 10 towel pullups. Lewis took his shirt off, briefly stretched his arms and then asked what the record was for pullups. Strength and conditioning coach Jerry Simmons informed him they were a new franchise, so there was no record.

Lewis jumped up to the bar and effortlessly pushed out 30.

"Jonathan Ogden was the first pick, but Ray took over the leadership from the moment he got off that bus," said Vital, now the director of college scouting for the Dallas Cowboys. "He elevated and changed everybody that worked with him – his coaches, his teammates. He carried the franchise to almost where it is today."

Taking charge

Lewis was so assertive in the summer minicamps that the Ravens released starting middle linebacker Pepper Johnson in early July. The message was clear: It was Lewis' defense. He flourished with 95 tackles as a rookie and a Pro Bowl berth in his second season.

"One of the first practices we had, we're doing a 9-on-7 drill. It was one of the first days we had pads on and [coach] Brian Billick was like, 'OK, this is a thud period,' " longtime Ravens defensive coach Rex Ryan said, recalling an incident in 1999. "We had this running back – Errict Rhett, I think is his name – and he used to run his mouth all the time. He runs through the line and Ray hits him so hard that it literally sounded like a gun went off. I'm like, 'God dog, I've never seen anybody get hit like this!' "

Lewis was already a three-time Pro Bowl selection when his career nearly ended in Atlanta in 2000. When Lewis returned to Baltimore and started preparing for the season, his legal problems mostly behind him, teammates and coaches noticed the changes.

"He was sitting in my office as low as any person could be," said Marvin Lewis, the Ravens defensive coordinator from 1996 to 2001 and the current Cincinnati Bengals coach. "He just turned to me and said, 'I want to learn the game how you know the game, I want to be the best, the ultimate linebacker who knows everything about the position.' That day, we just stood at the blackboard literally for hours drawing things up on the board. It was incredible. He was at the crossroads of his life and he wanted to make football full time, all

the time. That day was a major turning point in his life."

In the 2000 season, Ray Lewis led a record-setting defense that pummeled the New York Giants in Super Bowl XXXV.

Lewis doesn't talk a lot about his sports idols. He'll bring up Jim Brown and Muhammad Ali on occasion, and he has great admiration for Michael Jordan. It still pains Lewis that Jordan ended his career with the Washington Wizards and not the Chicago Bulls.

"The day Jordan put on another uniform, I made up my mind that I will never put on another uniform," said Lewis, who earned about $95 million during his playing career, according to Spotrac. com, which tracks professional sports financials.

Newsome allowed Lewis to test the market as a free agent in 2009. That's when Ryan was preparing for his first season as the New York Jets coach. His team needed a middle linebacker and he signed Ravens free agent Bart Scott instead.

"Whether he would have come with us or not, I don't know. There was no way I was going to do it," Ryan said. "Ray Lewis was and is the Baltimore Ravens. The fact he only played with one color jersey, that's appropriate. When you think of the Baltimore Ravens, you think of one person ... and that's Ray Lewis."

In Lewis' last game, the defense that had been the backbone of the franchise for most of his tenure staged a goal-line stand to turn aside the 49ers in Super Bowl XLVII and help the Ravens win their second championship. Two days later, Lewis' "last ride" ended on a Humvee traveling through downtown Baltimore, throngs of Ravens fans celebrating the team's Super Bowl win.

Saturday marks the five-year anniversary of his last game. The Hall of Fame announcement is on the eve of Super Bowl 52, the number he made famous. In those recent moments where he's retreated into silence, Lewis has thought long and hard about what it all means, especially to his family. He was raised by a single mom and has six kids.

"It's one of the greatest rewards I can give my mom. It's one of the greatest lessons I can teach my kids. And it's one of the greatest accomplishments I can share with Baltimore and Ray Lewis fans," he said. "I don't know if anybody will appreciate this moment the way I appreciate this moment right now." ∎

Baltimore Sun reporter Mike Preston contributed to this article.

Lewis elected to shrine in his first year of eligibility

BY JEFF ZREBIEC · FEBRUARY 4, 2018 · THE BALTIMORE SUN

Ray Lewis never put any limits on himself. Even as a young kid growing up in Lakeland, Fla., surrounded by poverty and crime, Lewis not only told his best friend, Kwame King, that he was going to make it out, he vowed that he was going to make it big.

The second of the Ravens' two first-round picks in their inaugural draft in 1996, Lewis set his sights on not just becoming an immediate NFL starter, but also becoming the best middle linebacker in the NFL. After establishing himself as a perennial Pro Bowl performer, Lewis promised Ravens owner Art Modell that he'd deliver him a championship.

Lewis learned Saturday afternoon that he can now check off another box and revel in the highest individual honor of a player's career. Exactly five years after he played his last game and went out as a Super Bowl champion, Lewis was elected into the Pro Football Hall of Fame in his first year of eligibility.

"It's so fitting from this perspective: You tear your triceps in October, right, and you fight your butt off to get back and I come out and I say, 'This is my last ride.' Nobody knows where it ends," Lewis said after the newest Hall of Fame class was introduced during the NFL Honors awards show. Lewis did his trademark dance after he was introduced. "Then, for it to end in New Orleans, for my last ride to walk off a football field forever a champion and then now to be here five years later and now to walk off a Hall of Famer, I don't know who else writes that story. It's the greatest story."

With Lewis regarded as one of the best defensive players of his generation, his selection was considered little more than a formality after he played 17 seasons and garnered 13 Pro Bowl selections and two Defensive Player of the Year awards, and won two Super Bowls, earning Most Valuable Player honors for the Ravens' victory over the New York Giants in Super Bowl XXXV.

Lewis has talked about how much it would mean for him to be elected in his first year of eligibility and how symbolic it would be to be voted in this year. Saturday marked the five-year anniversary of the Ravens' 34-31 victory over the San Francisco 49ers in Super Bowl XLVII, the last of Lewis' 249 career NFL games, including the postseason. The announcement also came on the eve of Super Bowl LII, or 52, the number that Lewis wore with distinction throughout his Ravens tenure.

"I think the most important thing was family for me, to see Mom, to know the story, the journey. And I dedicated my entire career, my life to her and to share that moment today, it was different," Lewis said. "Me and all the guys were talking about it in there because it's this moment of finally giving Mother something that now I can rest. Right. I've been gone a long time. Now I can finally rest.

"I want to go fishing with a cigar now and just sit back. I don't want to work out every day now. And the second thing is growing up as a child, I know what that looks like, Mike Singletary, Dick Butkus, who dreams of being that category, sitting with those guys? And to walk up there today and see all of those guys walk up there it was the most amazing thing ever to be mentioned with these guys and now we'll be family for life."

Lewis will head a star-studded 2018 Hall of Fame class that also includes wide receivers Randy Moss and Terrell Owens, middle linebacker Brian Urlacher and safety Brian Dawkins. Former Houston Oilers linebacker Robert Brazile and former Green Bay Packers offensive lineman Jerry Kramer also got in as senior finalists and ex-NFL executive Bobby Beathard was voted in as a contributor.

Now 42, Lewis will become the second homegrown Raven to be enshrined in Canton, Ohio, joining offensive tackle Jonathan Ogden, Ozzie Newsome's other first-round selection in 1996.

"For 17 years, we could point to No. 52 and tell the other players: 'Follow his lead. Practice like Ray practices. Prepare like Ray prepares. Be a great teammate like him.' It was our privilege to have

Amid the towering flames that accompanied his heralded entrance on game days at M&T Bank Stadium, Lewis brings the Lombardi Trophy to the masses at the Ravens' Super Bowl XLVII celebration in February 2013. *Kim Hairston | Baltimore Sun Photo*

him as a Raven," Newsome said in a statement released by the team. "We are all better for having him here. His play on game days speaks for itself. Even in that small group who have the honor of being a Hall of Famer, Ray stands out. When you talk about the great players of all time, no matter position, he is among the greatest of the great."

Lewis attended Ogden's Hall of Fame induction in August 2013 and said that's the only time he's been to the Hall of Fame.

He'll have his induction day Aug. 4, and there will undoubtedly be hordes of Ravens fans who descend on Canton to take it in. Ogden was a generational left tackle and the best Raven on the offensive side of the ball for much, if not all, of his career. Lewis, though, has long been known as the franchise's iconic player, his name synonymous with the organization.

Years after he last played, Lewis still casts a giant shadow on the organization. A statue of Lewis in the middle of his elaborate pregame dance stands in front of M&T Bank Stadium, alongside one for former Colts great Johnny Unitas. Fans still come to the downtown stadium in droves wearing No. 52 jerseys and his presence, whether it's at a game or a charitable event in Baltimore, garners much fanfare.

"Ray represented Ravens football perfectly. He established what it meant to 'play like a Raven,' which has become a standard we believe in and our fans understand," Ravens coach John Harbaugh said. "It was an honor to coach Ray on the field and to maintain our friendship off it."

Lewis' passionate, hard-hitting and unrelenting style helped give a young franchise an identity that persists to this day. Lewis' legacy is highlighted by the two Lombardi trophies that are on display just inside the front entrance of the team's Under Armour Performance Center.

After selecting Ogden fourth overall in the 1996 draft, the Ravens essentially settled on Lewis, an undersized linebacker out of the University of Miami, with the 26th pick. The linebacker they truly coveted, Texas A&M's Reggie Brown, had been picked by the Detroit Lions nine slots earlier and Lewis was the top remaining linebacker on their board. At the time, the Ravens hoped they were getting a solid contributor to help anchor the middle of their defense. Lewis was much more than that.

He finished his career with 1,562 regular-season

tackles, 41½ sacks, 19 forced fumbles, 20 fumble recoveries, 31 interceptions and three defensive touchdowns. He's the only player in league history to have at least 40 sacks and 30 interceptions.

"Every time he stepped on the field, he was the best player on the field," longtime Ravens linebacker Peter Boulware said.

Any review of Lewis' playing career has to include his involvement in a post-Super Bowl XXXIV altercation in Atlanta that left two men dead. Lewis was initially charged with murder, but the charges were dismissed when he pleaded guilty to obstruction of justice.

The early 2000 incident made Lewis one of the most scrutinized and polarizing players in the NFL. His former teammates and coaches say it also spurred a shift with the linebacker, who fully devoted himself to football. He won the first of his two Defensive Player of the Year awards in 2000 and was the leader of an elite defense that smothered the Giants in the Super Bowl, making good on Lewis' promise to get Modell a championship. Lewis waited 12 more years to win his second Super Bowl title, his self-proclaimed "last ride" ending with a Ravens coronation.

Beyond any statistic, Lewis, he of the fiery pregame pep talks and unrelenting work ethic, was known for his ability to inspire and elevate those around him. Capitalizing partly on Lewis' success and the play of the team's defense, a plethora of Ravens defensive coordinators or linebackers coaches got head coaching jobs and solid but unspectacular defensive players landed big free-agent deals elsewhere.

Younger Ravens followed Lewis' lead, integrating themselves in his detailed film study sessions and his rigorous workouts. Safety Ed Reed was the Ravens' first-round pick in 2002, also out of Miami. He developed a close on-field relationship with Lewis that made the Ravens defense one of the gold standards in the league for nearly a decade.

Now, it's a legitimate possibility that Lewis and Reed, who both played their final game as Ravens in Super Bowl XLVII, will go into the Hall of Fame in back-to-back years. Reed is eligible next year.

"I believe my big brother is one of the greatest football players to ever put on a uniform," Reed said. "Everything he displayed about the game – on the field and off the field – by being a leader and a constant professional truly set a great example for those around him." ■

▶Lewis breaks out into his distinctive dance at the unveiling of a statue of himself outside M&T Bank Stadium in September 2014. General manager Ozzie Newsome (right) has said of Lewis, "Players are aware of his passion; they know he is the ultimate competitor." *Lloyd Fox | Baltimore Sun Photo*

Even among the greats to play his position, Lewis was a singular figure

BY MIKE PRESTON · FEBRUARY 4, 2018 · THE BALTIMORE SUN

Ray Lewis could have played in any era of the NFL, which is why he is the greatest middle linebacker ever.

There have been other great ones, such as the Chicago Bears' Dick Butkus, the Green Bay Packers' Ray Nitschke, the Atlanta Falcons' Tommy Nobis, the Kansas City Chiefs' Willie Lanier and the Baltimore Colts' Mike Curtis, but they weren't complete players like Lewis.

A lot of them wouldn't have been on the field on third down or in passing situations in today's game while Lewis never came off the field. He could easily cover a running back or tight end and was the first middle linebacker who could run sideline to sideline without losing a step.

In the era before him, most middle linebackers simply had to be agile from tackle to tackle. Like Butkus and Curtis, Lewis put fear in opposing players, and he took away their will to play against him. Just ask former running backs Eddie George, Corey Dillon or Jerome Bettis.

But what made Lewis even more special was his leadership ability. He practiced and played hard on every snap. He motivated his teammates, especially the younger players. He could do it with his performance or verbally.

"He might have been the greatest leader in the history of football," said Ravens Hall of Fame offensive tackle Jonathan Ogden, who was selected

Always looking to motivate and inspire, Lewis shares a Turkish proverb on the back of his shirt during Ravens training camp in August 2010 at McDaniel College in Westminster. *Lloyd Fox | Baltimore Sun Photo*

by the Ravens in the first round of the 1996 draft along with Lewis. "He could get people to follow him. He had that kind of charisma."

Lewis was a two-time Super Bowl champion, selected to the Pro Bowl 13 times and was named the Defensive Player of the Year in 2000 and 2003. He had a major impact on the game and became the model for NFL middle linebackers.

He is the best. Period. ∎